Letters
Never Meant to be Read

By:
Marc D. Crepeaux
Kristi Denker
Joel Dockery
Brandon Lawrence
and
Meghan C. Rynn

Curated and Edited By:
Marc D. Crepeaux

Printed in the United States of America
First Printing, 2016

Rusty Wheels Media, LLC.
P.O. Box 1692
Rome, GA 30162

ISBN-13: 978-0692815038
ISBN-10: 0692815031

Printed in the United States of America

-Disclaimer- Any resemblance to actual persons, living or dead, events, or locales is entirely coincidental. While some instances or thoughts may appear real, they are merely a perception of reality, brought to life by the letter writer. If you feel you have been wronged somehow as a result of this publication, feel free to write and send a letter of your own.

Have our paths crossed before this? I have loved, been in love, and certainly mistaken love for lust, or perhaps vice versa. Were we friend or were we foe? Real or imagined? Regardless, I have changed your life and you mine. Therefore, we write. I dare you…

-Marc

This is dedicated to those who feel lost in an artificial world.

-Joel

To my Mother: A realist who is never afraid to tell you the truth and always speaks her mind.

-Meghan

To my family: not just that of blood, but by choice.

-Brandon

Contents

Dear Reader,

*H*ave you ever wanted to write a letter to that guy or gal you brushed up against on the train? How about that lost love or the friend that did you wrong? A few years back, I started writing letters that I had no intention of ever mailing, snail or otherwise. This grew into a collection of very salty rants and unspoken melodies which I decided to put into a fine collection for the entire world to marvel upon. Then, I invited my sarcastic sister to join me in this endeavor and she wrote some of her own. After, I realized that this collection would not be complete with only our input so I started inviting other people to write letters as well. What was an exercise of the utmost fruition has turned into something very real. This fine act, turning an idea into something tangible, is one that gives me great pleasure and will likely continue until I someday walk the plank.

Ideally, I would enjoy more than anything to see letters pour into this publisher's PO box from all over the world, and to publish a collection twice a year. But alas, like all dreams, we must start somewhere. We must provide the spark for others to see the vision too.

This will be, with great hope, a continued collection

of signed or anonymous letters that span all subject matter. The writers never intended on mailing them. Some are heartfelt, some sarcastic, some are funny, some are revenge in words, and some are rants. They could be to anyone, even a letter to yourself. Rants or wondering what could have been can be healthy, so roll that sacred parchment in an airtight bottle and send it out to sea. Wait…

If you do have any letters, send them immediately to me. They will be considered for the collection and you will be compensated with possible fame and a bit of money, or perhaps even a small parcel of land in the Dakotas. Happy reading!

– Marc

Send Your Own Letters to:
rustywheelsmedia@gmail.com

-or-

Rusty Wheels Media, LLC
PO Box 1692
Rome, GA 30162

To My Heirs,

irst off, I want to apologize. In the event of my untimely death, you may find this letter wrapped in some of the newspaper that I tended to collect over the years, or in a window sill stuffed with blankets, or in a toolbox underneath the stairs next to the silver coins and those clips that I could never quite figure out how they worked or what they went with. Untimely death, what does that mean? Every death seems to be just at the right time and there is nothing any of us can do about that cold frustration, knowing you could be next. I suppose if you had a surprise death, that could be considered untimely for everyone else that is still there picking up the pieces, which is what you must be doing right now, picking up my pieces. How old should anybody live anyway? I was never much of a fatalist but I do believe that you were supposed to find this letter, so call me crazy if you must.

I wanted to apologize earlier for not allowing myself to make more money. Yes, I set the barricades, the traps, the pitfalls. I alone caused all the unfortunate circumstances. I no longer blame anybody else. At least I have that going for me. The changes that occurred over time to me, to my legacy, and eventually to you were the fault of no other, I bare that burden alone. The fact that I was likely found buried amongst my very important papers or *V.I.P.s* as I like to call them, willing and able to clean up my act but without any trace of instigation, could serve as a life lesson for those about to tread. I believe wholeheartedly that making more money could have solved some of my ailments, or even made them worse, chiefly amongst them, collecting.

Where did I start? Well, sometime in the two thousands I worked for a famous bookstore in New York City. I began in the warehouse because I failed to pass the author and book test but was able to argue for a job anyway. I weaseled my way into deliveries, the way I sometimes did, even though I didn't have a valid driver's license. We would go around the city picking up books that were deemed unwanted, oh those precious books of my youth, how much time spent between those legs, those hopes and dreams. Gold, they were like gold and I coveted every moment, every interaction no matter how difficult the stairs and load, no matter what pain or frustration the dialogue caused to my weird shyness.

There was one man who had an apartment which must have not seen many visitors except us book catchers, we were important, allowed to come in as guests of sorts. We were like henchmen hauling away rocks, powerful geologic wonders that our boss already surveyed. This man with few visitors created a small hallway, shoulder wide that some could walk through and the place was filthy beyond belief. The smell in the air, the mold would tinge your nose and keep with you for the whole day. There was a roach highway running through the open bathroom window which skillfully winded along the walls, the tiled floor, throughout the bathtub and into the living quarters, into oblivion. The roaches ran the place, the real show in there, and I'm sure there existed some kind of superior network that would survive any nuclear holocaust. There was a bed, yes, but something most would refer to as a biohazard of sorts, I'm still surprised that I did not carry anything home with me, or did I...

I never had as much as some growing up and possessions ruled the day in media of all kinds. They made you feel like you didn't have much. I remember saving up my lawn mowing money just so I could put on layaway that BB gun from Kmart. What a concept! Nowadays, I could get the gun and hold the burden of interest on the debt, but I sure could have the satisfaction of "owning" the piece of steel and plastic early and often, without the burden of afterthought, until the third or fourth bill came of course. I'm not inclined to blame the system, I'm not going to blame other people, but the system was born there, then, and it took hold of me with such brilliance that I became convinced that I needed those things in order to manage, to continue on in my oh so elusive pursuit of happiness.

Seeing that man's apartment in my early twenties changed me somehow. Is it changing you now as you look around and scavenge my home, your new inheritance? I don't remember the man, what he looked like or how he talked, but I remember his possessions and I remember his roaches and their network. The second touch was when I got kicked out of the Mexican family's home on 139th and Riverside in West Harlem and I moved to the barber shop owner's place further East and North a ways. I didn't really get kicked out; I kicked myself out, a financial and social move which allowed me to stay with my girlfriend unencumbered. I essentially moved my things into storage because my new roommate forbade me from staying there or opening the casket thing in my room, under where my bed would go which must have contained drugs sold in his barber shop. His name was Ricky, he had perfect hair and mustache, he was Dominican and I remember the time when I actually used his barber shop, my beard was trimmed so nice and shined, I should have maintained that look forever. He never said I couldn't stay there but my girlfriend at the time feared for me and I always stayed at her place further downtown for company. I always had a calling, just never the right one.

The friends I could get, four of them, carried all of my belongings from that fifth story walkup. We trekked up the thirteen blocks and over at least three avenues. It was just far enough that it made the journey a hardship, even for young men, but just close enough and at a weird angle that the subway didn't make any sense. I could have been rid of all of those things, those possessions, difficult to believe that I still have any of them now. That lamp, that Jason mask, those snowboarding goggles… I remember two of my friends carrying my mattress on their heads, stopping and starting, we must have looked crazy marching all that way. That same mattress I would never again sleep on, that bed that would sit on that drug coffin could have just been burned into nothing, could have been left for a homeless guy along the way, just kicked to the curb for the taking. I didn't need any of those things, whatever they were, but I employed my friends to carry them anyway. I even cut into my measly salary just so I could go and check on my possessions from time to time. I never stayed in that apartment, never even hung out there or cooked a meal once.

Like everybody else during my time, I likely spent half of my salary on things. I want to use a better word to describe them, but that is all they were. Cars, trucks, gadgets, plastic dreams for the kids, tools, everything needed to exist in modern suburbia. My meager salaries squandered over the years with dreams that tickled the same parts of my brain as the BB gun. I fantasized over the smallest object and how it would improve my life considerably, later forgotten and eventually thrown away or kept forever in abandonment.

We tried to keep up with the fast movement. I was quick to sell items too, finding a kind of enjoyment of rare finds of books, art, furniture, and old cars. I would have surely turned a profit but while I made something out of nothing, I was also paying debt with high interest on those items. The modern marvels of my day were all unhinged and put right in front of your face with no care at all, you needed this or that, and, you were going to pay.

The mini-malls that stripped the lands of green speckled every commute to nowhere when I moved to instant suburbia. This caused a psychological hindrance in my mind but I do not blame others for my own misfortune. The consumerism caused by my surroundings was a product of my own weakness. Flashy signs and lights garbled my brain into a kind of trance during long traffic lights with nothing else to look at. After a while, I had a hard time just staying home and chilling out. I always had to be somewhere, doing something, which meant buying something, either service or product, and that meant money down the drain.

After I got some of my act together, I bought my first house in earnest. I used my smooth tongue to strike a deal that most risk takers would envy but the majority of sane people would avoid. I bought a hoarders house, a pack rat's palace at a bargain in a good location, and proceeded to tear through another man's life. You will do that now, dear heir, tear through my life, as it were.

The agreement was not in his favor. The handshake and signed contract included an ambitious timeframe really when it came to his precious items and their inevitable removal by my ownership. Should he not be able to cherry pick the things he wanted in the allotted time, it would all be mine to do as I saw fit. Within the same timeframe, I was trying to remodel the house, serve as my own general contractor of sorts and I found things and squirrelled them away for my own profit and use. The man was not what I would call a pizza box hoarder, as I liked to say, but the offspring of a Great Depression and a Great War long forgotten. He, or his aging mother would see things on TV, buy ten, open one and use none, over and over. Tools, refrigerators, trinkets, Chinese wonders and late-night offerings of riches all filled that old brick ranch. Like the previously mentioned apartment with the roaches, there was a hallway throughout the place, shoulder wide with aisles of forgotten usefulness.

I tore through that house with no regard. Instead of using a scalpel, a careful surgeon, I was a bloody butcher with cleaver in one hand, machete in the other and I threw and gave away half of the man's worth with no care for his sickness. I opened the back yard to strangers who hauled away junk: old windows to remodeled trailers, jeep parts, bicycles, and the occasional useful hose or forgotten couch. I had my friends make piles as they went through and I would inspect what they took before they left. I should have charged twenty-five a head. The old man started collecting clothes and shoes for veterans, or so he said, which most never made it to their destination, their new owners. They never made it past the makeshift clothes hangers, with all the elastic gone, shoes dry rotted.

Even though I extended our agreement by thirty days, the previous owner still could not get all of the things that he wanted out of that house and would often be seen cursing, picking through one of the six thirty-yard dumpsters I had hauled away. His daughter privately thanked me for my efforts and patience. I cleaned up her inevitable mess. You, dear heir, are apparently not so lucky. I was the best man for the job at the time, my mind was not riddled with such a great hold on possessions, not like him anyway, and the proceeds went right back into making the house a livable palace.

New everything, the place was real cherry when I was done, most of the remodel brought to us by gold and silver found in the basement, rare but still cheap items sold on eBay, and the exchange of items for labor. I could have made more, been shrewder even, but I was in a race with the old man and his daily van loads of junk. He would even come get buckets of dirt, something he worked hard on over the years, that rich, mulchy soil.

I remember when I started with the remodel project in the back half-bath; the old man declared to me that all the guns, gold and jewelry was out of the house. I found that later to not be true in the slightest way. He had not a clue what accumulated in the rooms and large basement over the years. The ability to inventory mocked his aging brain until I reminded him of items he once longed for, wanted again, as I threw them in the many dumpsters without the slightest care. But there was something in his sickness, in his yearning that I too couldn't entirely slip from. I was made to, on several occasions, hold in my hand such items, weigh their significance on my soul, and cast them out into oblivion as a matter of course. Oh, how I wish I could do it all again, another chance to save those things for a bigger profit later, or make use of them, point to them to my guests and tell a story. Wait, that was it, that was how it started, take note.

Why newspapers? Why are there so many newspapers around you? Sure, I figured you would ask about the fire hazard. You are now likely standing there, ready to light a match and run. There is a bucket of them there in the corner. An old lady lived in a small bungalow down the street from my dad's house when I was growing up. She too had a shoulder width isle and towering stacks of newspapers, of history, of time. Why? I always wondered that, even when I began, forty one years ago to be exact. I started collecting the headlines because, as you well know, I was a writer and I saved clippings for story ideas. Police beats, outlandish claims, even want ads all filled my brain with notions of the real and unreal. Clippings became sections, sections became whole newspapers, those became stacks and stacks of… Well, you get the idea. The other rare items and gold I built as a fortress of solitude. Didn't notice me at those family reunions or the Christmas dinners, did you? Well, that's because I was here, with my things.

Have fun with the money, no really, have fun, make good memories. Be careful as you go through, as you hold things up to the light and weigh the consequences of keeping or no. My best advice that I could give now would be to light that match and run, be sure the insurance policy is well in place and just chalk it up to excess. The gold and silver will survive the blaze, some of the rare items too, maybe even that clock on the wall…here we go again. The possibilities on such items, such rarities are endless. I encourage you to simply cash out. The burden of those things, of that time and worry spent is far too great. If you are able to sell off all of this madness, for that's what it is, do cash in on the gold and the heirlooms, please do not buy other things with the proceeds.

This is my fair and stable warning. You have the inevitable chance of catching something here, probably already did. Your best shot now is to sell everything, mine and yours together. Cast away your worries, all that you own, and lie yourself on a beach somewhere with the knowing that you avoided a plague.

-*Marc*

Dear Fat Girl Pants,

Not the most glorious name. That's what you are though, fat girl pants. Tailored just for me, made to fit my fatty fat fatness.

Just so we're clear, I do not like you. You come up to the middle of my back and cover my freakin' belly button. Your tag says low rise. I don't know if there was a mix up at the factory or if I should be offended. When I wear you down on my waist line (where I originally assumed you'd go) my ass instantly becomes fifty years older. I do not think you're funny.

I'm working very hard to get rid of you. Ironically this means you've begun to look worse on me. Do you get some sort of sick pleasure from my saggy ass? Unfortunately I still don't fit into your prettier sister, Chubby Girl Pants, not yet. I will be done with you forever in a month, two at the latest.

I haven't decided what to do with you when I'm done. Should I keep you as a trophy? A silent unflattering reminder of what I've accomplished. We have a lot of history together. The bottom of your legs worn and ripped where I stepped on you one too many times, stained with years' worth of dirt, snow, and salt, the frayed stitches between your legs where my thighs rub together thousands of times a day, the one piece of fabric that sticks out of the top of your left side that I just can't seem to stop picking at.

I don't know Fat Girl Pants, maybe I would miss you. We have been through so much together. The only problem is, I learned a long time ago that good memories don't mean you're a good friend. I think you'd be better off with someone who fits you. You have a month to pack your shit and leave.

-Meghan

Dear Ivy,

I really enjoyed our time together. I have no hard feelings towards you and I hope you have none for me. You have to keep in mind that I was only nineteen years old and I couldn't have been ready to settle down like you wanted.

The first time I came to your place in the Bronx, the cab driver I hailed from the subway station was Puerto Rican and he asked me if I was sure I wanted to go to the address I gave him. I was sure. I have always been into new things and racial barriers never bothered me. Also, what is the worse that could have happened? I suppose the whole thing could have been an ambush but whoever would have got nothing, I had nothing. I actually didn't know that I had something until I went to your place that night and saw what it was like to live in the outer projects. You didn't have much, but you had an exercise machine you were proud of and said you used it often.

That was actually the second time we had gotten together, remember? The first was at my place in West Harlem. We walked around the Dominican neighborhood and Riverside Park, sometimes holding hands, sometimes flirting. It was amazing to me that you

13

called, considering I handed you a piece of paper with my name and number on it before getting off of the train at 125th street a week before. I thought you were Dominican and I thought about saying something sweet in Spanish to you before hopping off the train before my actual stop. I was getting my nerve up while peeping at you and figured I would hand you the note right after we emerged out of the tunnel and I could scoot out just in time to save any embarrassment.

Walking around West Harlem with you did ruin me forever with the Dominican girls in my neighborhood. They can be more racist than whites. I didn't care, you were wild and new. I was a little disappointed that you tried to wear club clothes though. It was your modest teacher's outfit with contrasting candy red corn rolls that really attracted me in the first place.

You told me later that when I first saw you on the train, you were coming back from a job interview you didn't get. I got to run my hands all over your spikey crimson hair later that first afternoon when we went back to my place. Hot afternoon sex with a seasoned black woman really spoiled me, the downtown college girls just didn't compare for a long time after that.

Even though it was far, I liked going to your place and being treated like a king. You would get a sitter for your two daughters, we would have our fun and then you would cook me breakfast in the middle of the night. You were a great cook and would do it all again when we got up in the morning. I obliged with some of your strange sexual requests too, I chalked it up to experience and some of it I was actually into and made other people do afterwards.

You were always trying to prove to me that you weren't ghetto. I knew you weren't, you were a school teacher and I held that with some regard, having no idea what it was like to teach in the projects. You were always trying to convince me that you exercised regularly too, even hopping on your elliptical to demonstrate once or twice. I never had a problem with your weight, you were beautiful the way you were and it's not like you were a compulsive eater or a slob by any means, just thick. I liked thick.

After about a month of random encounters and soothing phone conversations, I was playing it loose and you were planning for the future. What a crazy notion because I was getting pressure from my friends to go out on the girl prowl while you were conniving a nest and a way for you and your daughters out of the projects. You told your girlfriend all about me. You told her that I was big where it counts, kind, had some money, a good job, and lived in a nice neighborhood. I lived in a decent place over by the park which used to be a landfill. I paid six hundred for a room and some shared space which I would have considered a dump. You thought it was just great.

At thirty three years old and a mother of two kids, you failed to recognize that your oldest, age twelve, could have easily been my little sister, skin color aside. We were living in two worlds and you wanted a way out with a young white man who was a college dropout making nine bucks an hour at a bookstore in

Manhattan. It somehow seemed glamorous to you, the big ticket downtown. I know you genuinely liked me and we made a good bedroom team but you knew how my color gave me potential. Something you thought you would never have. I would never understand that very serious dynamic that plagues our country until years later.

I secretly loved you and I guess that makes me a tramp. I fell in love with everyone I met back then and I wanted to be the one to rescue you. I talked to my mom about the whole situation. She was only a tad older than you at the time. My mother had me young just as you had your first little girl. My mother listened patiently, without judgment but warned me of sinking my youth into someone else's problems. She was scared that I even went to the next level and met your daughters. That was not my idea but I remember taking them to the playground one Saturday morning after a healthy Friday night romp, knowing what I did to you in your bedroom. The day was nice, the breeze was good and they had fun. I have always been good with kids but I was thinking about your oldest daughter in a few years and me, fighting off the boyfriends from school and serving as some kind of role model. That brought me back to what we had just done when they weren't home. I was no role model, I was evil. They were just kids who didn't yet know their lot in life.

Sometimes I wonder if I'll get that phone call or a tap on my door because you have managed to track me down to tell me we had a son. A little mixed race kid shows up on my front porch with a school bag, tracking down his father, waiting to be rescued. You told me that certain tubes were tied after your second and I believed you so after the first few encounters, we went at it with no regard for making babies. That's how I preferred it anyway but it could have been a sweet little trap. I've learned now that people will do anything if they are desperate, especially a mother who wants something better for her kids. About the time when you started looking at apartments for us to split, I knew I could never see you again. It was immature of me not to discuss the impossibility of it all but I was barely a man. You should have known better because I sure as hell didn't.

That's not fair and I am sorry. I know you were desperate and were looking for something you thought you would never get. You grew up too fast and was a single mom trying to raise two daughters to not be like you. The whole situation just began to focus after listening to your voicemails which were growing ever desperate each week I ignored your call. Every Friday that went by that you didn't get a sitter and I didn't come over and you didn't cook me breakfast killed you more and more. You felt the rope slipping away. At the same time, a lover, another man walking out on you again. I know your oldest daughter's father was in jail and I know it must have been hard to tell people. I am sorry for abandoning you. I hope you understand that I was just too young. I wanted to fulfill the role that you needed but I just couldn't.

I saved your voicemails for a long time after, knowing that anytime I could just pick up the phone and head on up. I hope that you're ok these days and that your oldest made it to college like you wanted. I hope you met a nice man who stepped up to the plate and could give you what you deserved. I want you to know that I respected you and what you were trying to do with a terrible situation that was your life. I never thought you were trash.

–Marc

Johnathon,

*M*yyearbook.com was a strange place looking back at it. Now that I'm older I realize it was a free dating website, but at the time I thought it was like Myspace. You could quickly view people's pictures and "flirt" with people you thought were attractive, if they flirted with you back you were notified. You could cycle through fifty guys across the country in one day if you wanted. I'm pretty sure that's what happened between us.

It was a long time ago. Once we started talking it was obvious that we had a lot in common. I told my best friend at the time all about you, and she shared her adventures on the website. I always thought you were better. I remember rushing home every day after school and getting online to talk to you. Your profile picture was of you outside posing with a snowboard in full winter gear, which I thought was odd since you said you lived in California. You were tall and of Native American decent, which you pointed out multiple times.

I don't remember how long it was before we decided to exchange phone numbers, a few weeks maybe. Now that I think about it, I should have called you first. There weren't any cell phones at the time, so I gave you my parents' home phone number. About forty-five seconds later, the phone rang. When my parents asked who it was, I told them "telemarketer" and ran upstairs so we could talk. I was obviously a bad liar, because they called you back later that night.

Do you remember the story you told them? The next day you called when my parents weren't home, and you said, "Listen, I met you in New York." It goes pretty blank from there, my head was spinning. "My Dad is gonna kill me" Is all I could think. They knew I gave their phone number to a stranger, they knew I had no real idea who you were; they knew they knew they knew.

I got off the phone with you pretty quickly. My heart was racing, and I was praying that my Mom came home first. Luckily, she did. I was upstairs in my room. "Maybe everything went okay" I thought, "maybe everything is fine and I won't have to talk about it at all." Wishful thinking. My Mother came home and called me down right away. I crept down the stairs, my mind racing, how can I get out of this? "Meghan we called that number you said was a telemarketer" she said. I looked around the room, my faced shaped in a frown. "Okay" I replied "Well" She continued, "I traced that phone number and it said that person is a convicted sex offender."

This hit me like a truck. I went with the story you told me. I met you in New York through a friend. I only did this to avoid further confrontation with my father. I repeated the story you told, and they bought it. My parents agreed that it was okay for us to continue talking, and that they cannot blame you for your parent's mistakes. But I knew the truth. I knew it was all a lie. I felt stupid. Could I have really been talking to a pedophile the entire time? I deleted my profile that night.

About eight years later I received a facebook friend request. I usually just add everyone that requests me without thinking about it, this was no different. I clicked "accept" and moved on with my day. About an hour later I got a personal message from this person, it reads, "Holy Crap! I never thought I'd find you after you left Myearbook haha. I know you won't remember me, but you left a lasting impression on me there. It has been around 6-7 years I think, but every year on October 12th I try looking you up to catch up and talk. Hope you're doing well."

To be honest I didn't remember you at first. So I looked through your pictures and there it was, there you were, a tall young man with a snowboard in full winter gear. Could it really be you? Could I have been wrong all this time? I looked through your pictures and your profile. It was all a little surreal. Someone I thought was a creep turned out to be exactly who they said they were, just a kid trying to make a connection with someone on the other side of the country.

We talked for a while. We still seemed to have a lot in common. You told me that you lived in Georgia for the time being and you worked for a construction company. I told you about my job as a personal care aid. I mentioned that my brother lived in Georgia and maybe if I was ever down there we could finally meet, as friends obviously. We even talked about what might have happened if we never stopped talking. We talked about experiencing life together and growing old. It's strange to think about. I'm glad things turned out the way they did though, even after the pedophile thing.

I have to be honest with you though, you're the most narcissistic person I've ever talked to. When we first started talking, everything was fun, we swapped stories, and we laughed. But I slowly began to realize that every story I had, you had a similar one, only better. You bragged about going into college when you were a freshman in high school, but complained about being bullied in college while they copied your assignments. You boasted about your superior knowledge in everything, and made sure to use big complex words to prove your point. You also made a point to correct me when I was wrong on every topic "Actually Charizard is only 5'7" and about 200 pounds, I can't believe you didn't know that." You can't act like that and legitimately wonder why you have no friends and are still single.

All that aside, I'm relieved to know you weren't some old man jerking off to me on the internet.

-Meghan

To the Shadow,

Even in the darkest, blackest of nights I see you there. You're darker than anything around you. Are you there? And if so, what are you? Who are you? Are you a symbol? Are you my past? Are you a demon, a monster, or are you my dad? I hear you whispering to me. But what is it you are saying? Is it hate, is it rage, all in my name? Because I feel like I know you, in fact, I am certain of it. Your lack of a face is one I recognize all too well. You are him, the monster I escaped, and the thing I fought for so long. The very thing I refused to become. The thing I left back there, back where you belong, or so I thought. But yet here you are, every time I turn around. Every time I'm having a bad day. Every time I have a sip of alcohol, here you are.

You verbally assault me, again and again, just like you had for almost fifteen years. Hitting me, hurting me, breaking me down. For love, for lesson, for strength, for nothing. All the reasons I have been told in the past, but finally I truly have escaped you. I've escaped your words, berating, beatings and hate.

For a long time I took the very words you told me as absolute truth. I believed that you were right. I was nothing, I was weak, I was always wrong, I was broken, undesired, undeserving, I was worthless, a mistake. I was meaningless. A repeating list that never ends, ever expanding, ever changing. And although I had gone so long fighting you with the only weapons I had ever known, my hands, my mind, my words, my hate, and my rage, I realized something, something so incredible, almost breathtaking. It isn't forgiveness, for that is something that will only come once it is too late. But the greatest weapon I have, unknowingly, owned this whole time, is that of thanks.

Thank you for all the terrible things you have said and done. Because of you, I have learned the most valuable lesson of all. I have learned gratefulness for love. Although you had never showed it to me, or if you had, it was in your own sadistic ways. I have learned that people can still love me truly, and see through the monster that I am, the carbon copy of you that I am or I believed I was. But I have realized otherwise. Yes I am made from you, yes for the longest time I was you, but now I am so much more. So again, thank you, the Shadow that will no longer haunt me. It is because of you that I have learned who and what I truly am. I am me, I am unique, I am special, I have worth, I am able to love not only myself but others more than myself, I deserve only that of which I work for. The two most important things I know to be the true, absolute truth. I'm not to be controlled, but to be free. To fly and fight in my rightful place amongst the gods, I am not yours to sell.

And I know why you did it, why you hurt me. It wasn't the alcohol, it wasn't the hate, and it wasn't the guilt, it was fear. You were afraid of me because I'm not you, but better than you. Because I'm so much stronger than you, and that drew fear, as it should. But I will not take revenge upon you. That is an action that I no longer want. I won't make you hurt, like you have me. Instead I will prove that I'm better, I will show you that I'm better simply by being more of a man than you have ever been. By loving, cherishing, holding, supporting, and caring.

I will have a family of my own when I am ready. I will give my love and my children the world. I will never lay anything but a caring hand on the ones I love. You can remain the Shadow in the dark, but I will do everything in my power to be the light. One so bright, that when I shine you will appear nonexistent.

Thank you for showing me a hell that very few have ever experienced. It is because of you, that I will be able to settle for nothing less than heaven on earth.

-Brandon

To Those About to Marry,

You have ten seconds to tell me what you are doing. Can't do it, can you? Key words are usually uttered about love, the rest of your lives, the one and only, soul mate, blah blah blah. One out of a hundred of you, maybe, answered "entering a contract". The rest are entering a vague, metamorphosing, open-ended sentence that doesn't reconcile with a period but rather, death. Worse could metastasize: property settlement and division of your chattel, i.e. children. If you're lucky, you won't be falsely accused of sexual or spousal abuse, or end up in jail. You might, however, be imputed with the income of a budding Donald Trump for, of course, "the sake of the children", so that either Mom can live the lifestyle she prefers to be accustomed to and/or she'll treat her children to the loveless material affluence she never had.

It's not like marriage is a bad thing-we just tend to make it that way. Well-reasoned contracts with delineated responsibilities, contingency plans and exit strategies work all the time in business. That is the exact opposite of marriage. Even in my lifetime the very definition of legal marriage has changed, inclusive now of same-sex couples (but not triples, or more, because that would be unnatural). That is in addition to the radically different interpretations found in each country on Earth, and in each state, province, or territory. Take the U.S. for example-depending on where you live the "other woman" can get sued for "alienation of affection", but move to another state and they'll look at you funny if you try that shit. Property division in each state can morph as well-equitable, equal, whatever. The laws can also be applied as seen fit by a judge or lawyers.

Marriage can mean a different outcome for many people. It's not about love-love exists without marriage, and in most cases, it is more healthy that way. It seems to me that in so many instances, marriage is desired in order to avoid losing that love- it works about as well as focusing on that tree you're trying not to run into with your car when you're learning how to drive. Marriage kills love-instead of being held together with love. The participants become shackled by the implicit threat of cataclysmic change and destruction of family. A good marriage contract, though, can go a long way toward maintaining a balance of power and responsibility.

Nobody would dream of telling someone to bed their business partner, and only their business partner, whilst engaging in commerce under a contract that states that we are going to be partners and stuff, and make money and spend it, and have sex exclusively, if at all. Doubtful that Apple started that way, though maybe Woz and Jobs had a little side fling going on.

The solution I believe to be simple. Treat it like every other contract--well-defined and mutually beneficial, with a clear and spelled out exit strategy. If your future partner to be refuses to cooperate on that, well then, it is even simpler.

Say, "I don't".

-Joel

Dear Ex-Husband,

 here are so many unmentioned things you've done, said, and lied about over the years. There is one particular lie that pisses me off more than anything. I guess there are more that should piss me off, but people who know us both and have both sides of the story also know that you have lied so much that you don't know the truth from a lie. Know and see, that's all that matters.

However, this issue needs addressing. Granted, I probably will never send you this letter because well, I love the boys' momma (your wife) and can't believe she doesn't see right through you. Our boys on the other hand, thank God, do see through you and are not like you in this respect.

You were in basic training when your mommy wrote a letter getting you out due to a medical issue you lied about on paperwork, or conveniently left out. You never served, you never flew fighter planes, and you never saw what our real military has seen. You are not a vet, quit referring to yourself as one and quit taking thanks from people who believe your lie that you are one ...YOU ARE NOT!!! If I am wrong, tell me where are your dog tags, where are all your VA benefits? Why in the hell did we have to get food stamps and Medicaid as a family? Wouldn't a married couple get some sort of medical insurance through the VA? Seems everyone I know who served has insurance, obtained a VA loan to own their own home. I have never seen any proof that you served, an honorable discharge, no dishonorable discharge, nothing, no pins, chords, nothing, no fatigues (not the ones you bought for hunting at Army surplus). I'm talking about the Army issued ones.

By your claiming to be a vet, you are a disgrace to all our troops-past, present, and future. You are a disgrace to my fiancé who served eight years, to my biological father, my brother in law, my nephew who is still serving, to all troops and their families. There should be punishment for people like you but there isn't and that sucks. What you're doing is wrong and perhaps you should ask God for help with this lie and all others you've told for starters. Then perhaps rewrite your resume of life because you have more lies on there than you realize. I know this for a fact. No more taking Veterans' Day off, you're not a Veteran.

Always remember, a Tripod has three legs, not two. You never owned a Harley or were in any gangs. You never were offered a spot on the Dallas Cowboys football team. You never once traveled with any big bands or famous people. You are a dad who could never hold a job or stay in the same apartment very long.

I know I'll never send this to keep peace with my children, but trust me, they know the truth and how I feel.

-Kristi

Used to be Bestie,

*D*o you remember how we first met? It was 6th grade, we wore oversized cartoon t-shirts, and didn't shower regularly. We were introduced by a mutual friend on the playground, and then we were inseparable.

It's hard to remember the very beginning. So many things happened and it's difficult to pick a starting point. One moment in particular comes to mind though. I had my strange friend, Kimberly, she and I used to read books together and cast spells on rocks. You told me one day that I shouldn't be friends with people like her, that it looked bad. So we decided I shouldn't be friends with her anymore. You were the mastermind behind the idea so it was only fitting that you gave her the news. I hid in the green tunnel on top of the playground while you searched for her, when you finally found her on the field you said very simply, "Hey, Meghan doesn't want to be your friend anymore." To which she replied in a deep and melancholy voice, "Oh that stinks." She asked me later that day why I no longer wanted to be her friend. I never answered her question.

We went to high school and even planned on having a few classes together, like French. I wish I would have paid more attention, I really enjoyed French. Oui oui! We met up by our lockers every morning, and usually sat in the halls until first period. We'd gossip about the latest who's dating who and say hello to our other friends as they went by. We would text all class and sometimes meet up for bathroom breaks. I still feel bad about the day we stole that bag of lollipops from our substitute teacher in 10th grade, that same day you spit Gatorade on me from laughing so hard. There are too many stories to share, too many memories. Now that I think about it I did really well in high school after we quit talking.

We spent a majority of our time either at your parents' house or in my room playing games. We would take turns playing The Sims and Harvest Moon. When your brother bought a video camera we recorded everything. We made a few stupid videos and put them up on YouTube. There was *The Pizza Girl, Silent Killawog, The Genie,* and the one video where you came out of nowhere and started choking me. Replaying those made me realize how emotionally abusive you were toward me. Don't worry, I took them down a long time ago. Our music videos are still up if you ever feel like checking them out.

I dated a few guys and you were always supportive when they dumped me. I don't think I ever thanked you for being there for me through those break ups. It doesn't matter now anyway. You always seemed a bit depressed that no one ever liked you though. Honestly I think your standards were a bit high for the way you looked. No, not because you were fat. You didn't dress well. You didn't do your hair, or your makeup. Yet you chased the soccer jocks. Except for Kyle, you two dated for a week and then he dumped you on Valentine's Day. I think you cried about it for a few days. It was hilarious.

Everything began to change when you met Jordan. You guys started dating and moved pretty fast. I'm still convinced it's because you wanted to be able to say you did all those things before me. I feel like I need to clarify what really happened at camp that weekend. I've lied about it for quite a while now. But none of it matters anymore, so the least I can do is tell you the truth. Yes, I told everyone you gave Jordan blowjobs all the time. They all laughed too. They laughed and commented on how white your teeth were getting. I'm not sure if those two things are actually related or not. Want to know something else? I liked it. I like telling all those people your secrets.

The truth is you were a shit friend. You belittled me. You tore me down just to build yourself up. You used to tell me I gained a bunch of weight. You told me I was ugly, but don't worry, it was a joke right? I don't even think I was a real friend to you, just someone you could take advantage of, someone you could hang out with when no one else was around. I think you were embarrassed of me. It was a strange transition, but I'm glad you quit talking to me. It all worked out for the best anyway, I'm dating your brother CJ now, and I don't have to worry about your approval.

I may not have a lot of friends. And yeah, I gained weight. But at least I'm not a junkie working at Walmart, mooching off of 40 year old men in exchange for sex. At least I'm attempting to better myself while you go to parties and snort cocaine and smoke weed until you forget about how horrible your life is. You cry and complain about never having enough money, that you can't afford to pay your Victoria secret credit card and countless others, yet there's always change to buy booze and weed. It must be hard living at home with your parents while they cook and clean for you. It must be hard having them take care of your dog for you while you go see your "friends" for days at a time. Is it difficult being handed money whenever you ask for it? Your life must be rough.

It's unfortunate because you don't even realize how good you have it and you treat your family like garbage. Your oldest brother came to visit us all from Texas, weeks before getting deployed to a combat zone overseas. How much time did you spend with him? None. Not even a second and he's the only sibling you have that even gives a shit about you.

I want to share a story with you. One you were present for, but I want you to hear it from my perspective. Picture this, your parents about to depart on their dream vacation. A vacation they have worked countless hours of overtime to save for. A vacation they had to delay because of *someone's* self-inflicted health issues a few years before. A vacation spent just shy of two weeks, exploring the beautiful cliff sides and cities of Ireland.

They departed early Tuesday morning. I wasn't sure what to expect the first night. CJ and I went to the gym and returned late that night, probably sometime around 3am. The house was trashed, beer cans everywhere. Your parents shot glass collection was raided, used for bottom shelf whiskey left to rot in the sink. You obviously had friends over, three sets of sandals lay scattered around the dining room. Honestly I didn't care much about that. What bothered me was that you left the house a mess, and that you lied to your mother. You told her you were going to be at your boyfriends all week.

I heard a loud rumble shake the living room and a humming coming from upstairs, your parents' air conditioner. Maybe they left it on by accident? I went up to check. I found you and your friend sleeping in your parents' bed. Out of all the things that happened this probably disturbed me the most. It's just a strange thing to do, very dirty. Who in their right mind would want to sleep in their parent's bed? I can't get over it. You played this night on repeat every day after that: eat, drink, smoke, sleep in your parents' bed.

You left your weed and grinder out on the coffee table, probably forgotten in your drunken haze. You were clearly smoking inside the house, you used one of your mothers glass bowls as an ashtray, and left a few cigar filters on the table. Don't get me wrong, I'm not against smoking, but doing it in the house is disrespectful. This is what that entire week and a half boiled down to, Respect. Something you are severely lacking.

CJ and I went camping for a few days after that. I was glad to leave. We returned a day early due to unexpected rain, and as we walked into the house we found you in the living room. The house smelt like smoke. High and probably a little buzzed, you said something along the lines of, "I thought you were going to be gone all week."

To which we explained it was only supposed to be a few days.

Wheeling the cooler into the kitchen I noticed you had managed to eat a considerable amount of my food. We chose not to talk to you about this to avoid confrontation. As you know, CJ and I had to move back home due to financial issues. We paid about sixty dollars for all the food you managed to get your grubby hands on. We had our own fridge in a room and area you had no reason to go into. The funny thing is, if you would have just asked I probably would have let you have it. That is not what happened. Day after day I found my food, or lack thereof, eaten. Wrappers stuffed in the overflowing garbage can you neglected to put a bag in. One day, I found my cheerios out on the counter and I lost it. I wasn't allowed to confront you directly. You can thank your brother for that. So, instead I wrote on the cereal box "Don't touch our fucking food." Later that evening, I went to the fridge and noticed you had replied to my cereal memo, "I didn't have any, Assholes." This infuriated me. Not only are you a liar, but why were you back there in the first place? I wrote on the box again, "It doesn't matter, I said don't touch. There's <u>NO</u> reason why you or anyone else should be back here." I will admit that this entire situation was petty. But I was fed up. The next morning CJ woke up to a text message from you stating something like, "I only ate one hot dog (wrong) I didn't think you would care." (Also wrong) And you gave me the most ironic threat I will probably ever receive, "If Meghan wants to swear at me, she can swear to my face and see what that gets her."

All of these issues aside, we chose not to speak to

you. We didn't want you contacting your parents and ruining their vacation.

Your parents returned home around 11pm after traveling for about sixteen hours. We sat and laughed, listening to them gab about their wonderful vacation. I'm glad they had a good vacation. You were out of the house during this time. After listening to your parent's stories and looking at all the pictures they took, we told them everything you did. Your mother was furious. Even better, ten minutes after we had ratted you out, you came home with the friend you had been sleeping in your parent's bed with. I don't think I had ever witnessed karma that instant and beautiful. You said, "I didn't think you were coming home until tomorrow." You really need to work on your listening skills. CJ and I left the house so you could receive your punishment. I haven't spoken to you since.

You're name has always been ironic to me, you're nothing but a black cloud on that family.

-Meghan

P.S. Everyone knows how you really lost all that weight.

$\mathcal{D}$*ear Denton,*

I wish I could have been there to stop you. Anyone would have tried but I do think some of your friends or family would have been unsuccessful. It sounds so cliché to say that but it had to be said. Being realistic, I believe in survival of the fittest and I know that you just weren't meant for this world. It can be perceived as heartless but you weren't very happy so off with it anyway.

What was going through your head when you purchased the gun from Wal-Mart? It is like any form of consumerism I suppose. You shopped with a smile on your face and asked to see the gun behind the counter. You may have been so happy that you didn't feel that tight pressure when you handed over the money to the cashier. I can imagine you whistling your way back to the Cutlass and prying the cool steel from the cardboard in the cab like a young boy getting a new action figure. I imagine you peeling away the packaging with such intensity all the way home, in that incessant multi-tasking way you always had. I can see you smoking like a chimney, your last few, or did you already quit? Rolling down the side of the road, knowing the spot was already picked out many times before. I can see you pulling over and loading the gun, or was it already loaded when you left the parking lot? Were you crying? Did you cackle like you always used to or were you resolute? I wonder if your last thought was your crazy mother, your crazy girlfriend or was it just music in your ears? Did you pray? Were you high?

At your wake, your mother was completely hysterical and she told me you loved me. I find that hard to believe because we hadn't seen each other in years. She also said something I still don't understand, that you were already in heaven. I thought that blasting yourself in the face on the side of the road meant that you were definitely going to hell. I asked another Catholic once and he gave me a confusing answer. He said that if you were able to ask for forgiveness between pulling the trigger and actually dying, you were good. I find this scenario more likely for someone who missed and dies in a hospital bed surrounded by family a few days later. But you didn't miss when you shot yourself in the face.

Every time I see a beauty of a guitar, I imagine you standing there smoking, telling me how you could modify it or how you could give it a romp. I remember when I got my loan while at school and we went out shopping by where you lived for music equipment. We took the same Cutlass Cierra you shot yourself in and loaded it up with live show gear. I know, I know, I should have bought recording equipment instead. I thought I was going to be a rock star. The thing is, you could have been one, even if it was medium scale in the new industry.

I am always reminded of you by the painting *The Old*

Guitarist by Pablo Picasso. I'm pretty sure you loved that painting and I find it interesting that Picasso painted it after his friend committed suicide.

If you are in heaven or are a roving ghost, the least you could do is give me some insightful advice or scare the bejesus out of me in order to get me to change my ways. I must be doing a decent job of it though, no one that I know that has died has visited me yet but I wouldn't mind hearing your sarcasm again.

I remember leaving my shirt in your room on purpose after I took a shower, knowing that whatever girls you had over would get to see me come into the room all nonchalant, look for my shirt and just throw it on. Kind of funny because I am porcelain white but it worked at least one time all the same. She was too young and I was too stupid to follow through but I remember her and she remembers you.

Thanks for helping me find my place among the muck and the history and the pretentiousness that was Purchase. You helped me branch out and I didn't feel so bad about being so green. It was great to go to your house during breaks and play guitar and get stoned and talk about women. We had a great time hanging out with the nerdy girls of that suite and pretending to be so depressed and in pain.

The problem was, you were never pretending.

–Marc

Dear Broken Hearts,

I fully understand the destructive force that is a broken heart as I am sure so many people in this life do. And for those that have yet to experience such pain, I'm almost envious. Sadly, it is another one of those twisted experiences of life that at one point or another we all have to deal with. That one who cared nothing for you whatsoever, the one that cheated, the one who told you that you weren't good enough, the one that used you for personal gain, the list seems to go on and on, each time unlike the last.

I suppose that is because no two situations in life are exactly the same, no matter how similar they are. Along with the fact that each time it happens, it hurts worse. The heart is literally one of the strongest muscles in our body. Scientists and medical professionals believe this to be true for the simple fact that it is constantly being worked to provide blood to the rest of us. And of course this fact is indisputable. But I truly believe it to be the strongest for another reason as well.

When our bones take too much damage, they become brittle, they break or crumble. When our other organs take too much, they burst, fail, or just simply wither. When our mind takes too much abuse, it snaps,

45

and we lose our personality, our psyche, our sanity. But our hearts? They show that no matter how fragile we really are, we are almost as indestructible and resilient as we feel at our apex. For no matter how many times a loved one cuts it, beats it, rips it out and blends it into nothingness, our heart never skips a beat. It goes until it is our time to pass. Until then, it carries on.

And as beat up and hurt as you are right now, or as you have been in the past, or will be in the future, I believe that we can all learn so many valuable lessons from our heart. Most important is that, no matter what happens, we will be okay. Life will be okay. And with enough hard work, determination, and time, like our hearts, we will also heal. We will find more, so much more. All we have to do is stop taking out all the pain that someone else has caused, onto the very one that wishes to heal it. Appreciate every moment spent or seemingly wasted on those that left, and think of it as an irreplaceable experience, but also as motivation to keep going, to keep looking, and to keep our hearts open.

Just because there's a tree covered in rotten apples, doesn't mean that with enough time looking, you won't find the perfect one. Love is not a sea full of plenty of fish. It's also not a sea full of sharks either. Yes, there are billions of people out there looking for their one. But the amazing thing is we all have one. We are just so rushed into finding that person. Or we're so crushed by all of the terrible experiences we've had in the past that we fail to see. Like anything else in life, love takes persistence and work.

All I want for you, for myself, for everyone is the

experience of what true love is, what it feels like, what it looks like, what true happiness is. Keep your head up and cry as much as you need to, talk to whoever is going to help you feel better, dry your tears, and smile. You are beautiful, you are strong, you are resilient, and you are desired. Don't overlook those that comfort you.

All too often, we get so busy looking at all the rotten apples on the branches that we fail to see the perfect one right in front our face the whole time. Keep your mind on your heart, and keep your heart open. You'll be amazed how much brighter the sun will shine.

-Brandon

Girl with the Red Dreadlocks,

You bother me.

We all get it, you are skinny and have a nice body. Congratulations. Now please stop wearing backless shirts and lace... everything. I don't want to see your ass crack. I don't want to see parts of your nipples all the damn time. And I don't want to see your perfect, flat stomach. Do you actually get any attention from wearing all the nonexistent fabric you own? As far as I can tell everyone down at the corner ignores you eighty five percent of the time. Unless your prancing around and shaking your ass to get a free cigarette. Charming.

You're stealing my mojo. I'm supposed to be the pretty girl down at the corner. I'm supposed to be the girl that turns the guy's heads with my charming good looks and knowledge about video games, Lord of the Rings, and other miscellaneous geeky things. So go away. Your making me look bad... Bitch.

I guess the good news is that I don't do drugs, and I also find the time to brush my hair.

Love,
Meghan

49

Dear Nakita,

I know you can't read this, I know you will never be able to. But I hope this letter finds you in some way. Perhaps in a better place.

Do you remember when we first met? It was almost six years ago now. I was a different person back then. We both were. I'm pretty sure I was afraid of you, I think everyone was. Not too long after that I gave you a chance. Do you remember taking naps together in the boiler room when I had breaks at work? I think I enjoyed those more than you. You had a lot more energy back then. When I started my senior year in high school I was excited to do more hands on work, and I'm glad I got to do it with you. Just so you know, I had to pull a lot of strings to make that happen. So I hope you enjoyed it as much as I did.

I remember the way you used to look at me through the window in the door. You perked right up, sometimes you even danced. You always made me smile. I used to duck under that door when I had to leave so you didn't have to watch me. Things were so much simpler then.

Do you remember the first day I brought you home? You were a nervous wreck, breathing so heavy I thought you were going to pass out. Everything turned out okay. You learned pretty quick to call it home.

Everything was perfect back then.

You used to help me in more ways than words can describe. I hope you know that. Things never used to be so perfect, not until you came along. Your story always spoke to me, I can't really describe it. We were so similar. We needed each other. To this day I still believe I wouldn't be here if it wasn't for you.

When I moved again and left you home, please know I had every intention to get you back. I spent hours searching for a place to live. You spent a week at my newest apartment. Things got pretty bad. He just didn't understand, it wasn't anyone's fault. So, we moved you back to the house. It was for the best, and in your best interest. At least that's what I told myself. I'm still not sure if I believe it.

How long did you wait for me? How many hours did you spend looking out that window hoping I would show up? I will never forgive myself for all the heartache I caused you. I became the person I tried to save you from. I'm sorry I abandoned you.

I can tell you don't love me the way you used to. Please know that I still love you. I love you just as much as I ever have. Back to when we played out in the yard with Jack and ran in circles until we couldn't breathe. Back to when you used to steal my spot in the bed, then get mad when I would cuddle you. I will always love you that much. I hope you can love me like that again someday. I wish things would have worked out differently. I wish I could have been a better mother to you. But I'm glad we got to spend the time together that we did.

Love,
Meghan

Dear Mother Prostitute,

You don't know who I am and I don't know who you are but you offered me something years ago near Bruckner Boulevard in the Bronx. Your son was there too, about five or so at the time and he stood within ear shot and his innocent eyes looked at me with fear as I approached. That boy saw things that no youngster should see before and after our encounter near the bleachers of that little league baseball field. It was late, I was half drunk and the train stopped short like it sometimes did so I had to fearlessly walk over the bridge those last few blocks to get home.

I might have taken you up on your offer, all legal, decent, and moral factors aside, if you hadn't said something that still haunts me to this day. I was so surprised that this normal looking woman with a boy had offered such a thing for fifteen dollars, my only recourse was refusal. After initial proposition and denial of services, you said, "You sure? I'll suck your skin right off." Ughh, nowhere in that offer can I find the stuff that gets me going. I was more frightened for you, for me, for your kid by that statement than if you mugged me with a knife.

I imagined that little boy, not knowing what you

were doing with those men, what you would do with the money and where he would end up each morning. I wanted to invite you both over, I could find a snack for him and brew up some tea and we could talk about this. You had nice thick hair, milk chocolate skin and I wanted to save the both of you. I hope you are still alive and I am sorry I couldn't go to the bleachers while your son watched and I hope he is getting good grades in school and has a mother. I wanted to save you. Back then, I couldn't even save myself.

-*Marc*

To the Depressed,

It's both beautiful and sickening to believe that approximately four lives are brought into this world every second. In that same second, two lives were brought to an end. The average life expectancy is nearly 67 years old. To most that sounds like a long lived life. One full of: love, lessons (both easily learned and hard learned), riches (both sentimental and material), emotions, memories, events, etc. But with every event that occurs in our lives, forming the very memories we will love reliving in our minds, there is a person somewhere dying, fighting, and clinging to the very force that keeps us. And somewhere there is a person in pain, mourning the lost life of someone they love, longing to hold them again.

And then there are those like me. We long for the emptiness, the dark, the cold abrupt end. We hope that at some moment, either by our hand, the hand of a stranger, an enemy, or even one of a higher power, that abruptly we may be smited, struck down, punished for our doings, wiped clean of this god forsaken place. Where most fear death, we embrace the end to our misery, an extension of our pain in the form of our deserved religious-like hell. Or perhaps a seat amongst the ones we long for that we have lost, will lose, and the god or gods that we hold above ourselves. The fear of death in our minds is replaced with the fear that, maybe by some horrible miracle, we will live forever and lose everyone and everything that means the slightest bit of anything to us.

So while some of us cling to the knowledge that our death is inevitable and forthcoming swiftly. And wish for it to be false, nightmare-like dreaming. Fighting for the very essence and concept of life, there are some who are nothing but ungrateful for the fact that whatever caused our existence has cursed us with this thing we call life. And although these feelings aren't always self-inflicted or self-conscious, doesn't make us any less ungrateful assholes.

We need to realize that no matter what, it is near impossible that we are ever completely alone. No matter what, the very fact that we were granted life is a great honor. Our passing only occurs once we have served our purpose, our destiny within this world. No matter how big or small our purpose of life may be, we need to stop being so selfish, so self-absorbed, and begin to strive to achieve the reasons we are here.

Life is a gift and when we leave, what will happen? Someone will miss you. Someone will long to feel your embrace once again, only if it is earned. The only way we can earn that right is by going out of our way to be grateful and to embrace those around us no matter the means of their presence. Make a difference in their lives, and to help them make a difference with their lives. Embrace the fact that we are human. We are flawed, we aren't invincible, but we are resilient, and we are alive. So we need to live as such.

-Brandon

*P*CP,

*H*ave you ever spent longer than five minutes in your waiting room? The radio plays in the background while the children of meth addicts run around screaming. Cortland's finest. Every time I come here my phone's battery is always low, nothing left to look at but people picking at their skin, and medical magazines. I find it strangely difficult to look away from the products of crank and irresponsibility. Do they exist just for the tax returns?

Thirty minutes later the nurse calls my name. She walks me to the scale. I always set my purse down and make a joke about not wanting to weigh more than I have too. She usually doesn't laugh. Afterward we go into the room and she takes my temperature and blood pressure, never says if it is good or bad though. I guess I don't really care anyway. Next come all these ridiculous questions about my mental health.

"Have you felt depressed in the last week?"

"Sure."

"How often?"

"I don't know."

"Less than half, more than half, or every day?"

"I guess less than half."

Fifteen questions later she leaves saying you're running behind today, but you'll be in as soon as you can. You're always running behind so it's really not surprising to me. I politely say "Okay, no problem" As she closes the door. I think its awkward sitting in a room by myself. Sitting on that hard table covered in paper that's supposed to be a barrier for all my germs. I twiddle my thumbs and look around, informational posters, hand sanitizer, medical magazines. What is it with you people and those boring magazines? I like to look through all the cabinets. I never take anything; it's just fun to look through other people's things.

An hour or so later you finally knock on the door and slump your way in. You always seem so miserable. Do you even like your job? You're always ready to rush through everything, get the information you need and get out. You could at least act like you gave a shit about your patients. Trust me I don't want to be here either. We exchange few words about my progress and you begin clacking away on your laptop. I always thought it was awkward sitting around waiting for you to get done, so I decide to make small talk.

"I like your tattoo." I say and point to your foot.

You raise your eyebrow at me and look at your foot. "What about it?" you say, and keep typing.

Rude.

"I think we need to increase your dosage to 175mg." You finally say.

You always tell me this. I didn't pay a forty dollar co pay and wait almost two hours just so you can give me more drugs and push me out the door. Why don't you ever want to talk to me about the issue? Don't you think you could get a better idea of what the best treatment options are for me? But what do I know? I'm not a doctor. Oh wait, neither are you.

-Meghan

Parents of America,

You are awful. It is clear that you have no clue what you are doing and I have a hard time considering you brethren. That is not a texting kind of word so I assume that we should just move on. You have gone and let the world shape you, made you remold the way you move as a parent. Your kids are no longer happy to have a stick and a book to play with. They are no longer satisfied with your tender loving care and a pack of warm memories tucked neat behind their belt as they run off to school. Narcissism doesn't count as parenting. All real sense of community is blasted out of this world. The attempts made to replace it with virtual equivalents only strive to mimic the same sense. It does not work. Do you even know your neighbors in the cul-de-sac that you painted picture perfect?

These children should have been raised as you see fit, all antiquated and full of your hard-earned lessons and moral values. Messy, child-rearing should be messy. After, society could come in during the teenage years and combat all that you had taught them with the new and the brave, making a good, solid mixture to take on early adulthood. You don't have any hard-earned lessons or moral values do you? Not anymore? What happened? Were you born in the 80's? Did they get taken away or did you exchange them for the newest I-phone?

How many hours per week do you work, both of you? Oh, I'm sorry, is there a both of you? No, that isn't quite fashionable. Do you work and work and work because you must, because they need things that only you can provide? Sure, one can only blame you so far for the rat race. The problem is, you never recognized the race for what it is, out of control.

Daycare and commutes, salaried jobs without defined time limits, the children need this, the children need that. Pushing your child to read early will not make him a genius, similarly an early intervention does not doom your child to stupidity. What they need is a good strong spanking, some open terrain and the resiliency to move on, lesson learned. What they need is the knowledge of difference in a material world. They need not squeezing by pythons or the familiar glow of absurdity that is television. What they need is to be taken on an adventure, by you. Then, they need to be free to experience their own kind of quest. They need to eat real food.

If you coddle them, buy them whatever they want and accept everything determined by the Jones family for you, the result will be a child who fails to leave the nest on time and blames you for all their shortcomings. Do not keep your adult child's schedule in your personal day planner. You will see an American economy void of youth and innovation. We are already seeing the results come through now and they are ugly.

-Marc

Dear Children of America,

Y ou have been misled. Work is a four-letter word but it is not a dirty word.

Let me be clear on what I mean by work. It's doing something for others and getting money in return. It's so much more than that though. It's our chores, those things we do regularly to keep our stuff in good working order. This includes doing laundry, vacuuming the floor, washing the dishes, mowing the lawn. It includes doing things to build our minds, such as going to school or reading books. The effort required maintaining healthy relationships with our friends and family is also considered work. All of this can also be called maintenance. Volunteering is work too even if you don't get paid.

In this nation it used to be common for children to work in the fields and in factories for very long hours. In much of the world this is still how it is. Here though, we long ago abolished most child labor because of some problems.

You may have heard your parents complaining about work and how they wish for a bunch of money so they wouldn't have to anymore. They may have even thrown around the word "lottery". It's no wonder that many of you think work is a bad word.

Money is important and working to take care of basic needs is a necessity. Beyond that, there are many good reasons to work.

Working for someone either as an employee or in your own business gives you a sense of being part of something bigger. It's good for your self-esteem to see how your efforts are useful to the well-being of others.

Taking care of things you made or bought with money you earned shows respect for yourself. Your stuff will last longer and be more useful if you maintain it. This will save you money. Developing these habits and accepting them as part of the process of living is something many people never learn.

Putting effort into your relationships takes a lot of work. Many people think that if they feel love for someone, then everything will work out. That's not really how it works. You've got to exert effort to keep it balanced and healthy. The work here is to be a friend without trying to own or control the other person. It's very difficult to understand what exactly you need from another person and what they need from you. Most of the work of being a friend or family member is to listen without thinking of what to say next. Friends don't usually need you to do their thinking for them. It might sound too simple, but sometimes all that someone needs is for you to shut up and let them express themselves, and that's hard.

-Joel

Dear Teachers,

I'm writing this letter to vent on your policies, your curriculum, and your attitudes towards your students.

Policies for being absent or late: Well, students arrive via bus basically the same time every day, pending roads, traffic, weather, and no issues with said bus. Children that walk or who are brought to school? The same timeframe holds true, providing no unexpected car problems, or issues at home. So, teachers should take attendance at the same time daily, not whenever.

Policies for being sick differ daily as well. You send home a guideline, yet you yourself don't follow the guideline. You send a child home with a temperature of 98.9 and yet we are told to keep them home if higher than 99.9, which is it? I can tell that you count sick absences against the kids without a doctor's note but not every cough, sniffle, upset stomach, vomiting episode, or headache warrants a doctor visit. A bug is a bug, a cold is a cold. Not every family can afford constant doctor visits to appease and satisfy your policy. Leave parenting to the parents. Half the time we don't even know when our child has visited the nurse at school unless they tell us. If my child is seen, I deserve a note or a call. Let me be the judge if they need to come home or be sent back to class.

The Common Core crap sucks, we can't help our children with homework because we learned math a simple, easy, and no nonsense fashion. This new long, drawn out, stupid form of math makes about as much sense as trying to mix oil and water. As far as homework goes, you have our kids for eight hours a day. If you can, put your cell phones down, stay off your computers and teach them what needs to be taught. Maybe you need to rethink your lessons. Most households need two incomes to make ends meet and the only time families have together is in the evenings. I'd much rather my child's brain take a rest and enjoy evenings as a family than have them putting more hours into homework at night.

Last of all, I am sick of your attitude towards students. They are children, first and foremost not a $, so stop looking at them as such. You get money for each child in their seat? Well that's great but parents and children don't want to hear it. If a child is not there for whatever reason, I'm sorry you lose pay for that. Really, shouldn't you be concerned if Jane is sick or she was not there because she was beaten by her drunken dad the night before? Maybe if you all took the time to see that Bobby was bullied so much by other kids while you were too busy worrying about a text or email, or what money you lost because he isn't there, you might just discover that something is preventing a parent from sending him to school. These kids will not grow up with the education they need and deserve if you don't realize the problems may actually be the school, the teachers' attitudes, and conversations between you and other teachers the children can hear on the playground.

This probably makes no sense to any of you but my mind is going a mile a minute and I can't keep up with my thoughts. Pick it apart line by line, like you do the math problems now, you can figure it out.

-Kristi

Dear Amelia,

We were young when we broke free. The river had consumed us. We spent years fighting him off. When we finally killed him, I think it was a little bitter sweet. We spent so long fighting, it's all we knew. Where do we go from here?

We did many things when we were young. We lived a thousand lives. We sailed the great seas and explored the ends of the earth. We lived among the animals. For a while we thought we were animals. We were there for generations. Mating season came and went. We watched the young grow into powerful leaders and succeed their parents. Do you remember when Rex attacked? Many orphans were made that day. We spent the next few weeks building the orphanage. Things were rough then, everyone was scared for a long time. We got through it though. Sometimes I wish we would have never left the jungle.

As we got older we split up. I went to explore what treasures the hill had to offer. You were forced to stay at the top until your training was complete. I missed you for a while. It didn't take long for me to notice a change in us after we separated. Our relationship changed, you changed. We spent so many years running away from men, avoiding them, killing them if we had to. Suddenly it was all you could talk about, men. You lost your passion for adventure and exploration, replaced by an infatuation with the opposite sex. It took many years before I understood this feeling. I still crave the thrill of our escapades to this day.

I revisited the fort not too long ago. We worked so hard to repair it. We stuffed mud in the cracks to keep the cold out, painted the walls, and left our hand prints forever marking that point in time. I "cooked" food for us, and you took care of the critters we collected. Neither of us were very good at our jobs, a lot of amphibians died in that old shack. It's probably haunted.

In case you're wondering, it looks very different now. The windows are broken and the harsh winter and rain was not kind to our old sanctuary. Mold covers the couch and cupboard. Our list of critters to collect and study deteriorated. The locks have all rusted. I can't remember the combinations anyway. The spiders have taken over, not that that's new information. It still smells the same. I could never forget the smell of rotting wood, rusting metal, and wet dust. I don't think I want to. No matter where we went or how long we stayed, we always came back to that place. It was our home.

We lost touch for a long time. You chased men, I chased destiny. But fate works in strange ways. You found your prince, and I had found mine. You've been at the bottom of the hill for some time now. We nodded when in each other's company, but nothing like we used to. One day we were forced to travel together. The season had just begun and we unknowingly decided to travel to the same destination. It was on this day that we became friends once again.

We never adventured together after that. No, our encounters involved sitting by the fire and reminiscing of the good old days and planning new ones. Luckily for us, our princes quickly became friends which made meeting up even more enjoyable. Those days were short lived I'm afraid. It seems my prince and I weren't meant to be, my search would continue. Not too long after I left the valley, the bottom of the hill, I had taken all that it could give me so I left. I left to find my next adventure somewhere far from that place.

We lost touch for good it seems after this. You found a palace to call your own, even started a family. I'm happy for you, truly. But it doesn't seem possible to rekindle this flame. We are too different people I'm afraid. Drawn together by the blood we share and the memories we've created.

-Meghan

Dear Prospective Employer,

Yes, I have achieved things. Yes, I can do your no frills job with satisfaction of everyone in your petty, cramped office. I maintain the ability to sit there at nausea, waiting for another satisfactory human to complete a mundane task thereby handing the baton to me while strutting, late as usual, so I can take the "project" that last leg before it goes to the big boss.

I want to thank you so much for peering at my resume and giving me even the slightest chance at getting a job. I have bills to pay, after all, and they keep mounting. They call for my heart to be ripped out and served on a silver platter among others in a nice long row, still pumping and bleeding for sure. We do want to avoid that. What have I been doing since my last job? I can tell you. I have been paying one bill off with another down the road to include hefty interest. I have been using plastic as if it were real money, funds I actually had. I have been screwing my future self to the wall of shame.

I perfected the art of my resume, skewing the truth here and there to get past your robot gate guards who scan lives for key words and phrases. I even paid someone with debt to make my rap sheet just so. I have fooled your coded keepers this time for sure and can only say that it is all there, see it? See all of my degrees that nobody cares about but everybody said I should get? My apologies, I have too much education for you. Do people with degrees make you squeamish? See my previous work experience, even the times when I went out on my own and took a chance? Oh, you don't like those items either. They scream, "not a team player" for sure. I should have put something else in there, damn. I should have pretended just a little more, given myself honorary employee status during those years of failed entrepreneurship.

What happened to my past precious business ventures? Why do I no longer run that "company" or operate that personalized service? Well, I discovered, just as you know, that employees don't care. Nobody can afford to pay anyone to care. A "living wage" is a joke, a game being played like a carrot on a stick. Must use a fake carrot though, a real one would spoil, dangling there so long and that wouldn't do. There was also the issue of scalability. My big plan to never talk to people like you again worked for a time. Others got wind of this success and wanted to join which caused too many cooks in the kitchen, it happens. Also, such items as budgeting for growth and payroll tax aren't on a learning curve and my expensive degree programs didn't discuss pitfalls. That happens too. I learned quite a bit during those experiences, much more than the idiot sitting next to you in that cubicle who eats meatball sandwiches and takes twenty six minute breaks. So why not pick me? Why not take a chance on someone who knows what life is really like?

Perhaps I am being too honest here. What I need to do is lie about all of it. I should give my buddies the heads up, give out their numbers as my previous employers, gain true status. I could even offer them a sixer to make machine or copy room noises, hustle and bustle in the background. Oh, the heights I have risen to, but now it is time to come down from my perch and do some common good for this world, do some real work with you.

Or maybe all this time and effort I am putting into writing this and a thousand others would be better spent on something nefarious? Yes, I hear that criminal enterprises are always hiring and why not take a cue from the bill collectors anyway? Maybe I should just create a real leadership role for myself. I could better spend my time reading the paper. The police beat would allow me to build a team and put my skills to better, more profitable use.

No, that just wouldn't do. The risks are too great and what would my mom think? I suppose I should just settle for begging for that hourly wage you offer and the fringe of being by your side. I will do a good job, I swear. Not great, but good, and solid, real solid too.

I am desperate. I am alone, afraid of the future. I am naked, just as you wanted me. Take me now. I will do whatever you ask.

-Marc

Dear Foster,

First, I would like to discuss what should have happened. I invited you to come down here to Georgia to start a new life. I have a younger brother about your age, but since his life is already wrecked, I thought I would try and help a cousin. I only wish there had been an older someone helping me out when I was in my twenties. I fronted you the money for your gas to drive down here, repairs on your truck, and a month's worth of living expenses in exchange for labor on the hoarder's house that I bought. This is where you would live for the next few months, free and clear. All you had to do was log your hours working on the house, find a job, and possibly go to school. Pretty simple and easy considering you were making ten dollars an hour, commuting thirty miles one way and living with your mom. After laboring off your original debt to me, I would pay you what you were making but without taxes and a commute. There was so much work to be done, even if I was not there telling you what to do every hour, the labor needed was obvious.

The goal here was that you would have from October to roughly February to get your act together, find a steady job, and move into an apartment while my family and I moved into the repaired hoarder's house. I was offering you free housing in exchange for some labor. This is great considering when I was your age I moved to New York City into a six hundred dollar per month room with only three grand to my name and desperate for a job. Back then, it was survive or go home with my tail between my legs. I actually made it through and lived there for many years, played in a band, and eventually found a blue collar yet lucrative job as a doorman at a real swank hotel. Can you imagine if I had four months head start to live for free? This is a college town and jobs here are easy come, easy go. All of this seemed pretty cut and dry and while I was called away for uniformed duty for six weeks, you had ample time to find a job without me coming around finding more work for you to do around the house.

I gave you a bed, various creature comforts, a roommate for company, and a free internet connection. Now, let's discuss what really happened after you arrived.

All was well in the beginning as you started to settle into your new home. There were only a few weeks before I had to leave for training. You needed to become acclimated with the area using me as a guide. Your new roommate could help you with geography. I spent a good amount of time getting to know you a little better, mentoring you, and helping you find possible areas for work. You worked hard alongside me, and we kept good records of the time spent so you could chisel away at the debt I paid getting you down here. Everything was running along smoothly. I was a little alarmed by your eagerness to set up your X-Box and your lack of organization, but I was willing to chalk that up to the norm of your age and generation. Things really took a turn for the worst after I left.

You had a difficult time finding work, but you had an easy enough time finding a source for marijuana. As I have told you before, I have nothing against the sweet weed; I just am not allowed to smoke it anymore. I don't care if other people do, as long as it doesn't affect me, and as long as they can still be productive in this society. Smoking all day every day is counterproductive for most people. It does not matter how "normal" it makes you feel or how much you think you need it to function.

When I came back from service, you had eight weeks of living in your new location, little was accomplished. I had even left you a list of things to do around the house and a dumpster to fill with the junk which was abundant. To my surprise, the dumpster was not full and few hours had been logged each week. I would have been happier had I owed you money for overworking instead of you still owing me money from your initial move. We had a long, hard talk outside, early in the morning after my return. Steam was still rising from the ground and much to your despair; I was back to smoking tobacco cigarettes.

I made you cry that morning in the fresh Georgia sun and steam. You were lonely you said, and you worried about your future. You should have been worried about your future; you had just squandered almost half the time you had to live for free. Since I am smart, resourceful, and know how to use a computer for things other than Facebook, I had already researched your options regarding school. The various technical, two year colleges around my house had already passed deadlines, even for the spring. I introduced you to another school nearby with an unconventional schedule and made you go look up their programs. Later that day, I drove you to the school which was within walking distance from my house and sat with you in the admissions office, took a tour with you, and left when the time seemed right for you to make your own decision.

A few hours later, you walked back to the house with books in your hand, beaming from ear to ear, saying that you started class tomorrow. You were so proud, and I was proud for you. Things were looking up. All you needed to find was at least a part time job and everything would be fine.

I convinced you to sell your rusty Chevy truck. Insurance had been depleting your savings, and you could walk to school at least from your current location. This proved difficult as it was a northern vehicle and had a great deal of rust. Who would want to buy a salty, rusted truck in the south anyway? Not a lot of takers, but this one guy kept stalking you and trying to trade an El Camino for the truck. It became a running joke with this guy, and even I enjoyed bantering with him over the phone. He was the one guy in Georgia who wanted your truck. I made it clear to you that you needed money to buy yourself an apartment and time, not another car. It was your truck, your decision, but time was still ticking on your free housing. When I wasn't around, you traded the truck straight up for the El Camino. I couldn't be angry; you were so proud of your new fortune, and it really was a sweet ride. Only one problem, you couldn't afford to register and insure it, so no driving except to switch driveways when contractors came to work on my house. You barely had money to feed yourself and went back to your woe is me attitude. The world was against you.

Christmas came, and you couldn't afford to go home, so I invited you to come along to some of my family events. We all had a pretty good time, and people liked you. Some of my extended family even bought you gifts. Your parents sent care packages, your mom baked you cookies, and times were decent enough for your first Christmas away from home. I was constantly driving you places, having you over for dinner, and buying you food. I didn't mind doing this, you were family, and especially if it meant that you would eventually succeed.

The holidays passed and your attitude for finding a job went south, but at least you were showing success in your studies. I wanted to move into my new house by my birthday in early February, and as promised, I gave both you and your roommate a month's notice. It became apparent to me that you would have no place to go so I made an irrational decision and paid for a full bathroom in my basement with my credit card so you would have a place to live. I wanted two hundred and fifty a month, with a nonrefundable security deposit of seven hundred dollars to help pay for the bathroom which cost around three grand. You used some of your tax refund money to help pay for the deposit, and I allowed you some time to pay rent with no interest. It would have taken a year of you paying rent to me to match the cost for the bathroom and other improvements, but it helped with the value of my home, so I was willing to adjust. I didn't really want you living in my house; it was my small family's first, and I expected you to be out on your own. But I would have hated to see you need to move back in with your mother since you were enjoying school so much.

We all moved in together as one happy family; you helped me take care of my dog, and time passed. Now that I was done for a while with the service, it was time for me to find a job. I told you mockingly that I bet I could find one in a matter of weeks before you could. I did. I actually quit one and found another while you found none. We discussed several business ventures including a live bait shop, but it was obvious you didn't want to do any real work.

My wife only complained a few times about your loud music, and you complained about the early morning stomping from my wife and two daughters getting ready for school. You decided to let me sell your X-Box on EBay. I thought the profits would be used for rent but one day you woke me up from a nap after a long day of work to complain about your life and your decision making and demanded I give you the money from the sale of the X-Box to buy food. You wanted me to feel sorry for you, and I did, so I gave you the money.

You wanted me to stop lecturing you like your father and belittling you, but I assured you that I was not talking to you like you were an idiot; I was talking to you like a man. This was the first time you showed me your pitiful anger, yelling with my six year old daughter in the house, so pathetic. You were desperate and ready to blame everybody but yourself for your problems. I am an optimist and was quick to point out that things were going alright, not yet terrible. You were going to college, you had a place to live, and you weren't out on the street. There is something about your generation or age, just behind mine, that believes there are things in life that are automatic and somehow owed to you regardless of your own decisions.

Since I no longer adhere to this outrageous philosophy, I proceeded to talk to you man to man, explaining how poor decisions lead to negative consequences and the world is not out to get you, despite your paranoia.

I then convinced you that the best thing would be to let me sell your El Camino on EBay. It would fetch a better price there and you could buy a scooter which required no insurance or registration and have money to start paying me rent and buy food. It sucked, but you finally agreed, and we changed the title over into my name since you were incapable of doing some adult actions yourself. We discussed and agreed to terms, which included paying the auction fees with the profits and I would take a small commission for my trouble. About that same time, I was bringing you around for interviews, and you eventually found a job at a fried chicken restaurant, not bad for a college student new to the area. You still agreed that selling the El Camino was the best course of action, and I would drive you to and from work when I could until you bought a scooter.

After declining for quite some time, your life seemed to steadily climb uphill, and I thought you were finally going to make it here. That is, of course, until you launched your progress straight off a cliff, and I got a call during my lunch break from the local police department.

Since I worked four in the morning until one in the afternoon, my lunch break was usually before you ever got out of bed. I would come home for "lunch" which usually consisted of eggs and bacon or cereal if I was pressed for time. It had taken me awhile to find Apple Cinnamon Cheerios again, but I was just about to pour the milk into the first bowl in a long time when I was interrupted with a call. The local police knew the location of my work and were actually looking and asking for me there. I must have passed them on the way out for lunch. They said they would be over in a few minutes and asked about you, whether you were there too, and if I could meet them outside before talking to you. I went outside with coffee and a cigarette, thinking they busted you with some girl smoking pot on campus or whatever.

The cop looked at me rather strange and asked if we looked alike. I told him we were cousins, both being tall, white, and bald so yes, we looked alike. He then asked me where I was at eight in the morning. I told him that I was at work. What he told me next caused me to ask for a repeat and when he did, I dropped my coffee cup, causing the copper to jump in his driving boots and clutch his gun. He told me that the nice old lady across the street witnessed you pleasuring yourself at the end of my driveway, naked, at eight that morning, traffic whizzing by. I was dumbfounded, I couldn't believe it. I thought they must have the wrong guy, or you were completely inebriated.

Grain alcohol, crack, LSD, sleeping pills; any of these could explain such actions. Five or six police cars showed up, and they all first thought I was the guy based on the description blaring across the radios telling the crime of the month in this southern town. A nice black police officer, the second on the scene, asked about weapons readily available to you and asked if I would go get you. I was so shocked that I went around my house and opened the basement door to find you, not remembering that police are like vampires. They just assume they can come in if you don't speak otherwise. They all followed and all I could say to you was to inform you that they wanted to talk to you. I stood outside with an obese detective, and he explained to me as they cuffed you and led you out of there that they found drug paraphernalia from pot in there. I did my best to act surprised and not guilty. After all, I had responsibilities.

When the big show was over and you left in a squad car, the jolly detective gave me his card and told me what would happen next since you confessed to the crime. He said that you were really lucky that despite the presence of two schools on my street, a child had not seen you. Otherwise, you would be facing a child abuse felony.

I had to call your mother. I didn't have her number, so I called my father. He didn't have it so I called my step-mother who gave me the number I already had that didn't work. So then I called our grandfather. I had to tell him what happened, and then I called your mom and told her what happened. She was frantic and blamed me for the whole thing somehow, and I could tell she didn't know what to do. I called my father back and explained to him the situation, hoping he could talk sense into his sister. I then remembered I was on lunch from work, and I called my boss and they figured I was in jail or something because the cops were there looking for me earlier. I assured them they weren't looking for me but a "tenant" and that I had some things to take care of, but I would be back to work soon. My boss was cool about it and told me to take my time and if I needed to take the rest of the day off, that would be fine too.

My head was reeling, I got in my car and smoked the tires back to work, only to turn around and come home. I called my boss back and told her I would just come in tomorrow. I went back inside and ate that damn bowl of Apple Cinnamon Cheerios.

I didn't even want to tell my wife what happened for the shame of letting such a creature into our house and our life. I had two young daughters, and I am so glad I never left you alone with either of them. This was so out of the blue, so I went down and tore your room apart to find a reasonable explanation. A vile and syringe, an empty bottle of moonshine, LSD paper, or magic mushrooms would have explained all of this, and I could somehow let you back into my life. I found nothing, the police found nothing but some small evidence of marijuana use. I was devastated and scared all at once. I feared the things that you did when I wasn't home, breaking into the rest of my house and rolling around naked in my bed or trying on my daughter's underwear. This episode didn't just put you as a criminal in my mind, but a different kind of human altogether. You proved that you couldn't control yourself sexually, and that made me fearful of you. I have known perverts in my lifetime, and I do not have any fond memories of anything to do with them. Rapists and pedophiles are the only criminal category that I still strongly believe the death penalty should be used for. You, cousin, had just lumped yourself in that very same group of evil.

You became dead to me. I didn't want to clean up your room or remember you at all. I only took one call from you while you were in jail, and I tried hard not to be furious over the phone. A representative from social services called me and asked if I would post bond and let you move back in; I told her no. There was no way you were ever going to be able to live in my house, never again. This flabbergasted your mother, she is off her rocker too, wondering why I was so upset and "he would never do this," that line of bull. All that time wasted mentoring you, helping you, paying for you, adjusting my life for you, gone. Time is nothing I could get back, but I would donate no more. I tried to visit you, even scheduled a viewing but I never showed. I couldn't face you and would rather you were dead. Not many people get on the dead to me list, but you were surely one of them. I couldn't get my time back, but I sure as hell could get some money.

The auction proceeded that week as planned and I sold your, legally my, El Camino for three grand to some Canadian who thought what a great adventure to fly down to the south and drive a piece of American automotive history back to Canada. He let me try a Canadian cigarette which tasted awful. I paid off EBay for the auction and thought about keeping all of the money. Your mother told me not to bail you out with it but to put what was yours in your bank account for later use. I kept what you owed me for rent, what you owed my neighbor, and I kept a little extra for a big word called restitution.

Although effectively keeping half of the profit didn't make me feel any better, bear in mind that I did have to go around to my neighbors and explain what happened and how it would never happen again and that I was sorry. I also had to miss a half day of work and explain to them why the cops were in there looking for me. I had to explain to my wife what happened, and no restitution in the world could have paid for that but my father warned me of Karma and suggested that I give you half the profits, so I did. Half was ready to do whatever with in your bank account when you were released.

For a while, I waited ready to assist you with your next stage that didn't involve me, but the great state of Georgia wanted to make sure you weren't totally crazy, and they kept you around for quite some time, despite being only charged with a misdemeanor. I gave up waiting, and when I had to be in uniform again, some hours away, you were released. I couldn't pick you up due to just plain geography, and your mother was so pissed at me. I saw the results all over Facebook, your family's favorite pastime, as it recounted the great tale of their son's homecoming. It was as if you spent the better part of spring on some grand adventure in Africa and had to narrowly escape the clutches of a ferocious lion in order to come home.

You were some kind of hero, and there was surprisingly no mention of jerking off at the end of my driveway for the old lady across the street to see and photograph while she was sipping her morning tea. Never mind wasting my time and energy on you just so you could pull some perverted stunt and blow it all away. Things were looking so good for you, you finally had your head above the water. You and your mother blame me for your problems, and I get random text messages from you asking where this or that trinket is like I stole your life. I wonder why you never asked about the money? I suppose you know you did me way wrong financially and you were just happy to get something out of it. Or, you needed something else to complain about and someone else to blame for all of your failures. It is obvious that you and your family would rather forget the whole thing and blame me for your heartache and your laziness, and whatever else caused you to go naked in public.

I feel sorry for the world the next time you do something of that nature for not recognizing you for what you are, a pervert, a loner, and a future predator. These may not be fair accusations but I am still living at the house which I own with a family which I love, working hard. You are back to living with your mother and telling everyone at my sister's graduation party that would listen what an asshole I was and how I stole money and an El Camino from you down in Georgia. Again, you failed to mention the incident at the end of my driveway to anyone. Your shame, mine too.

So while I have mailed you things that I missed when your mom and step-father came down to get your stuff, I have never forgotten that you failed to apologize to me. This makes me even wearier of your existence, and I can go on living my life to the end, just fine, without ever knowing or hearing from you again. If I ever do see you again at a family holiday, I won't have any words for you, kind or unkind. You are obviously unaware of your devastation on my life as well as yours, and I fear you for that. It is very difficult to get on the dead list, and some are even allowed to come off over time, you need not worry about being one of them. I would like to forgive out of my Christian heritage, but I see no point in forgiving a narcissist. You are dead to me, and I will never mail this letter.

-Marc

Dear Sadness,

*W*e've been friends for quite some time. For as long as I can remember, even as a child, you were there. We were acquaintances then but quickly became companions.

I used to hear your whispers in the back of my head. You'd tell me that no one liked me, that I didn't have real friends. They were all pretending. It didn't take long for your poison to set in. I believed every word you hummed into me. This noise was comforting.

There are many people that used to mean the world to me, some of them still do. It's your fault the rest are gone. I lost a lot of real friends because of you. You were never a real friend to me. You're a leach, a parasite. Chosen as your host, you bled me dry of everything enjoyable in life. So why are you still here? What else can you take from me?

I've tried everything I could think of to kill you. Pills, a long list of pills. You never left. You were only pushed to the background. Your song becomes quieter but what is remaining for me? A broken, lonely life. Sometimes I miss the soothing melody of your song. No, I refuse to wilt and end up like the other souls you've added to your collection. I walked away from you a long time ago but I can still hear your screams from the distance, begging me to return.

I knew I was always different. I didn't laugh at the jokes people made. I barley laughed at all. It didn't matter if it was a family member, friend, or stand up show on TV. I didn't laugh, I still don't. People notice but I try not to let it bother me. When I'm asked about my hobbies, it's an awkward conversation. I don't enjoy anything anymore, I guess I have you to thank for that.

I've spent a majority of my life in front of a screen. I didn't have to interact with real people. I could live the pretend life I had always wanted and shape it in my image. I was cool, popular, and successful. I've stepped away from that life, I had to so I could start a real one. I'm doing it, and I'm doing it without you. It's a strange and difficult transition, that's okay though. I'll find myself one day.

-Meghan

Dear Rhonda,

I wrote a much different letter a few years ago, a much more angry and spiteful letter. A letter I'm not proud of, at the time I meant every word. But I've realized a few things since then, so I'm writing a new one now.

I know we were never close. To be honest I don't think we will ever be, and I'm okay with that. Maybe our relationship never had a chance. You are twelve years older than me after all. Or maybe we are just two different people, oil and water. If the opportunity ever presented itself I think I'd take it. At the very least I'd peek my head through the door.

We still had a few good times. Do you remember playing dominos on the floor when you lived in the farm house? How about the time you wanted to sleep in and I wanted to watch a movie, and you let me pick out any movie I wanted. I picked Steven Kings "It." I was scarred for life, but you were the coolest sister for letting me watch it. I still get uncomfortable when my feet get too close to the bathtub drain.

I know we don't get along anymore. In my opinion we tolerate each other more than anything. I want you to know that I'm not mad and I don't blame you for the choices you have made. I know you have a lot of emotions and thoughts about what happened, I know I do. I like to think you could talk about them to me if you wanted to without it resulting in conflict. We share a lot of battles and I think it would be nice to be able to talk to someone about it who understands. But I'm not writing this to talk about the past.

I'm proud of you for graduating, becoming a nurse, and I hope you're happy in your career. I've heard being a nurse is stressful, sick people freak me out, and they complain too much. I could never do that job.

I guess what I'm trying to get at is you deserve to be happy in every aspect in life. Don't be afraid to change the things that don't make you happy. We will always be here to support you. Remember that.

Still afraid of clowns,
Meghan

Dear John,

This is not an *I'm dumping you* letter, it is a letter explaining what my heart desires from you as the love of my life.

You first and foremost complete me. I Love you for all you are, all you do, all you represent. You swept in and melted a very broken and lost heart, you made me realize I was loveable and could love again.

You and I began to build our Love from the ground up. You tried so hard to keep the romance alive and you did great. We spent a lot of time working on our home, our family, and our relationship. I was in complete awe. You were excited to see me every day after work, very excited. We were like teenagers sneaking around. You kissed me deep and full of passion. We made love all the time and then one day it stopped. It all stopped.

I wonder, is it me? Is it something I did? Are you regretting us? Is there something I'm not doing that I should be doing? Is it my looks? Is it my body? Are you not attracted to me? What is it? Where did things stop? When did things change? I know it's not my feelings for you because my love, feelings, attraction, and desires for you are stronger than ever.

We reached the comfortable phase. We've reached

the point where we really need to start concentrating on us. We need to bring the feelings, love, passion, and excitement back into us. Our children are getting older and making lives of their own. It's getting to be our time baby, our time to live and be crazy, do for us. We need to start dating again.

So I am sure you thought this was a *bye-bye, I'm over it* letter. It's just the opposite. It's my way of saying I Love You. I want to get back to where we were yet I also want a new us, the new adventures, a new found crazy love with each other. I want you to be excited to see me after work, to kiss me passionately, to have our romantic time together. I Want Us Back! We have many great years left in us and I want to celebrate. I don't need or want trips, cruises, gifts, or money. I want simple things: picnics, walks, talks, and cuddles-the Love I use to feel just by looking at you.

Let's Get It Back Baby,
Loving You Forever and Always,

Jane

Marty,

It's not that I was all that mad at you for quitting the band. I too had the sinking suspicion that the group was going nowhere anyway. That time that we were playing with our new Viking bass player and you came out to the show, I proclaimed "Screw Marty" over the PA during the set. I still remember and it was wrong. The sentiment may have been right but the timing and the actual words may have been a bit off.

The truth is, I knew that if you were there playing with us on stage, we would have been better and you were there anyway so why not? I felt abandoned like a kid whose parents get divorced yet he still sees both of them together on a regular basis. You were there in your passive aggressive way to make sure that we were still struggling and I'm sure you made comments amongst your group like "See? This is exactly why I quit" or "Marc is singing out of key again." I always sang out of key, I was still trying to find my voice. You could have served as a mentor but everybody was so antagonistic.

I am sorry for stealing the girl away early but in a huge way, I did you a favor. She was nothing but a year and a half of trouble. Thanks for introducing me to her but no thanks all the same.

I always tell this story which is a lie. One night, after our separate woman seeking endeavors, we met up and smoked a jay on some side street near Union Square. Do you remember? We saw this Asian kid all fucked up with tracks on his arms and asking us for money or whatever. We laughed at him as he passed out by a stoop with some garbage. That part of the story is true, as far as I can tell. Here is the rest which I use on occasion, maybe once or twice a year:

As we went our separate ways to catch different trains, I slipped on my headphones and started walking toward Union Square. I felt the hair on the back of my neck spike and I turned around to find the junky kid we were laughing at now lunging at me. Out of the instinct taught to me by my black belt step-father, I grabbed his arm in a bar and cranked it up his back. As he lay there screaming on the pavement, broken arm flailing about, I pondered what to do. I figured running was my best option but it might look suspicious. Then a NYU girl came around the opposite corner, frightened by the scene. I was there standing over this screaming lunatic. I saw her whip out her phone and call the cops so I got out of there and ducked to the subway heading north to West Harlem where I lived. The next week, I saw this kid begging for money in Union Square with a sling on his arm.

Pretty good eh? Did that really happen? By now, I have told the story in so many variations that I think it could be true. I do remember seeing that kid in Union Square wearing the same clothes like a week later. He's what I would call a stage two junky. His hair and clothes were still decent but would start to show some tarnish soon. He must have had a backstop, some people who loved him to death but I doubted if that crossed his mind when he stuck himself in the arms. I wonder where he is now. Maybe he is a father or leader of a fortune 500 company or he could be dead, who cares.

Remember Moose back in high school, that older guy that worked with us at the grocery? He had some problems too. Either we as a collective cared about people like that at one point or we just wanted to get some "adult weed", not sure. I do remember playing music in your basement and all the promise and all the talk and all the dreams. I wish both of us were better at following through with things, especially me.

Brick is a touchy subject because you came along during a summer break after it started and we had already recorded several albums. I came up with the name and the original idea so I am going to go ahead and announce to you and whoever else that it is mine. I did Steve and Benny a courtesy by counting them in on the copyrights of the first two albums. Just as Steve and I agreed, anything after that time should have called it something else. I did enjoy your input and playing together again, life was so simple and full of so much possibility. I just wish I wasn't stuck in my own head half the time, afraid to get out.

For a while, I will admit that I did feel like you were a storm chaser. I would get something cooking and you would come along to claim rights and play touch and go until it cracked. Some examples: Being cool, moving to New York City, the bands, and oh yeah, getting married.

We could have made a better team if we had each other's backs more, but in New York, life appeared to be dog eat dog when it wasn't. I have learned now that going it alone is far too sane and stupid. I still remember getting fish sandwiches on the corner by your apartment and how that tasted during the experimental phase two of our recorded music ventures, otherwise known as the rap/party music phase. I still hated you then for abandoning the band, but I was willing to let it go in order to foster something else. I just needed to find out what that was and you needed to help me, but it didn't happen. In a way, I blame your sad little roommate. He is dead now and I feel pretty bad not liking him when he was alive. If we all weren't so pretentious we could have had several bands going on at the same time, been cutting demo records every other week. If the guitarist and I didn't play so much Madden or I didn't get caught up chasing loose women...the list goes on. Regrets are hard because they stay with you.

When the apartment on Marcy got broken into the first time, I thought we all needed to be men and stand our ground and watch the place. I should have moved all my valuables to my soon-to-be wife's house and declare that I was out like you did, then I wouldn't have been out a Mac and the three thousand dollar credit card bill that came with it. I still remember you slamming down your last rent check on the bar in front of me and James and declaring it was your last. I thought you were a coward.

I do have to make a confession though. The morning of the first break-in, I worked the night shift and I came home and went to the basement and wrote a letter to my father. The door was open and either I didn't notice at first or I was just exhausted. While I was sitting there on your futon, a black kid in his early teens was pissing outside our basement door. I waited politely for him to finish before asking him what he was doing. He gave some hollers out to the street, what I later deciphered to be a signal to his watchman. He was breaking into our place but he hadn't gotten very far yet. The kid claimed that two white kids were running away from the apartment earlier with stuff in their hands which was total bullshit. I should have just clocked him on the head, tied him up and tortured him. I should have at least knocked him out and called the cops so they could take him away. I felt bad for the kid and wanted to believe.

He had to be the one who came back later after seeing all the great stuff we had and I could have prevented that and I am sorry. I felt worse for myself though because I lost out big compared to you. Those Hasidic landlords should be the ones to pay though for making mid-priced new apartments in the middle of the no income projects and marketing to naïve college kids. No, that is anti-capitalistic. Well, they should have at least put better locks on the doors.

We were all so young in New York and therefore, idiots. Oh, if I could go back and do it all over again. I would be patient, able to communicate ideas and squash conflict without it feeling like a full time job. I guess it's always like that, isn't it?

There is so much more to say to you. I am sure I will remember more after I seal this up and send it out to sea.

–Marc

Dear Cocaine Jane,

I definitely wanted to mingle with you between the sheets despite the fact that you were in that small social circle which included my girlfriend and some of her other kinky actress friends. You took me aside during a party and whispered the offering- the upfront prospect of us hooking up. This was deliberate and intentional, I was impressed. I maintained a careless as usual approach with regards to my social surroundings. I flirted back without whisper or regard, even blushed a little on the inside, relaying the notion that I too was up for a fling. I'm almost certain we were overheard by the hawks. I was a tad gullible and thought you might actually be into my young flesh until I realized that your little hot blond body was more into cocaine.

Right at about the eight minute mark, the batting of those blue eyes ceased, the thoughtless caress and laughter corralled. Horses actually chomped at the bit. You broached the subject of white powder and I began to realize that if I could portray myself as even a small potatoes version of a kingpin, you would let me do every dirty, awful, nasty thing I could come up with. Your body was a vessel for those kinds of wonderful acts and I liked the idea of strapping you down.

It crossed my mind a little that this may be a test by my girlfriend and I hesitated, already knowing the strange rock that would uncover, wings flying everywhere, bats. Wrath and bait, bait and wrath. It also occurred to me that you also could have a boyfriend. Was he here at this party? Oh, if he could see you now. That feeling gave me the chills, how chivalrous.

It was during that exact hesitation that you realized I didn't have the guts. Every guy has those cheating kinds of guts. No-it was the kind of guts to use coke as the ultimate aphrodisiac, the sexual yolk. That particular white baggy monster just made me grind my teeth and get mad at other people, a worry worry worry wort, so I put her down as soon as I picked her up. I never had much love for uppers in the first place. I preferred to smoke weed and go barefoot on the beach, settle my brain and have revelations. What would a guy like me do with a girl like you? I'm thinking long term here. Beach-walking, bed-waking, wife-making.

We could have come up with some sort of pimp arrangement, providing I could disassociate myself from you despite the love-making which would absolutely have to occur. Unfortunately, I associate love with sex and sex and sex so we would not have been able to work out long term, sorry. Unless I was supposed to save you.

Oh my! Was I supposed to save you? In that case, things could have been complicated and I would have ended up the victim-in need of a locksmith and a new pair of shoes. Standing on the moral high ground, somebody's daughter-skinny and ready to go.

I do want to thank you, thank you, thank you for introducing me to that breed of person who would change hands on a dime if a powerful drug they wanted happened to perch on another shoulder. My warbler is not as big as your falcon, but he has a best friend-a raven, and ravens are smart. I lost a great deal of trust in women after we talked and you took down my digits. I thought that someone besides my overprotective girlfriend was into me until I figured out what you really wanted, what you were willing to give up. This was simple math which helped me out for years after our spicy encounter. Thank you. Despite my live and let live attitude and my faith in humanity, I learned to despise your kind.

I am still waiting for you to call call call.

-Marc

To Those Who Need to Forgive Themselves,

To forgive is to stop feeling angry or resentful toward someone for an offense, flaw, or mistake. Right now I want you to close your eyes, take a deep breath, in through your nose and out through your mouth. Open your eyes, look at your reflection, or at least a mental image of yourself, and say, "It's okay, I forgive you for all you've done." You don't need some collar wearing man in a box to tell you you're forgiven for your wrong doings. You don't need some person to write to you, telling you you're forgiven for your actions. So I won't. I refuse, even if it just so happens that I am one you have wronged.

At the very end of our lives, we all die alone. And although we don't necessarily all live alone, at the end of the day you do have to live with yourself. So it really doesn't matter if those you've wronged or hurt forgive you or not. People come and go, through the ever revolving door of relationships that we ourselves pass through in the lives of others.

No matter your beliefs, reality shows that when your time comes you will have to own up to yourself, or to yourself and your higher being. Not them, not the victim of your offenses, flaws, or mistakes. They won't be there, just like they aren't there now. Don't you forget what you've done and don't dare try to justify or point the finger at someone else for what you've done. Don't pray, don't beg, and don't ask for forgiveness. Work for it! If you feel the need for their forgiveness, like I have, don't ask, show them. Prove to them that you deserve it.

But most important, use the choices of your past to model what you want your future to be, what you want the reflection in the mirror to look like. Take that dream image and create it from the core to the surface. Because that person is who you strive to be, that is the person you deserve to be. It doesn't just happen overnight, as I'm sure you already know. By remembering, holding yourself responsible, and by forgiving yourself is how you will change into this person.

Through experience, I have found that by first forgiving oneself, you're more likely to earn the forgiveness of the ones you desire it from. Change, adaptation, and evolution are the most concrete actions we have for achieving the goals we set. Even though you may not know me, I would greatly appreciate if you did me a favor which in turn will be doing yourself a great favor.

When you finish this in a few more seconds, stop what you're doing, even if only for ten minutes. Close your eyes much like I asked you to do in the beginning. Take your deep breaths in through the nose, out through the mouth. But this time, I don't want you to open your eyes, and I don't want you to say a word. Instead I want you to look deep down into yourself, find who it is that you are. Find the person you want to be. Grab their hand and pull them to the surface. Open your eyes and make that person your idol, your goal, and then work to become them. Because that person is the real you, and that is the you that is truly perfect.

−Brandon

Dear Brother,

My memories of you are few and far between, apologies for this letter being choppy.

I have vague memories of you as a child. You came to the house every other weekend I think. Sometimes I rode with Dad in the truck to pick you up or bring you home. I thought that was always exciting. I enjoyed seeing you. You used to greet me with a noogie, saying, "Hey, Goose." I used to enjoy this until I got older and needed my hair to be perfect. You used to say "Come here, I want to tell you a secret." Then when I got close you'd burp in my ear. I fell for it every time. One time you were in my room with me, I was playing with a dragon toy. His mouth used to open and plastic fire would come out. Do you remember convincing me that he would burn the house down? I sure do, I didn't touch that toy for months. Classic "big brother" kinda stuff.

You were gone most of the time though. You were going to college in the city. I used to help Dad pack your macaroni care packages. You sent books for Christmas for a few years, you gave me Lord of the Flies when I was in 5th grade and swore that one day I would read it in high school. I tried to read it, I really did. From what memory I have it was pretty decent. I was about eleven when you gave me that book. My comprehension level was far below what was required, probably still is. It didn't matter at the time because you sent it to me, it was special. I missed you a lot as a kid.

All those items you sent lost meaning after a while. All the silly gifts you sent me, like the "antique" bowling pin, were great but it was impersonal. It didn't feel heartfelt because it wasn't. This hurt me a little when I was younger. Maybe you just didn't care. For a long time I was convinced you didn't care about me at all. Then again, I thought this about everyone, so I'm not certain how much validity is behind that. Don't get me wrong though, I really enjoy our "Gag gift" Christmas now.

You found yourself a wife in New York I believe and moved to Georgia to be closer to her family. You had a daughter and visited every Thanksgiving. In 2010, Dad, my Mom, and I came to visit you. We had the same pair of black Converse. You showed us your home and around Atlanta. I had never been in a large city before, I did not enjoy it. It was too busy with five lane highways and a traffic light at every block, far different from what I was used to back home in the middle of nowhere.

The day after we arrived (I think) we went to the World of Coke. It was a little boring. Tasting all those different flavors from all over the world was fun and probably my favorite part. My Mom collected Coke items at the time, and when we got to the gift shop, she starting moving around, grabbing everything in sight.

I distinctly remember Dad saying to me, "We've gotta get your mother out of here before we go bankrupt." That still makes me laugh. They had the polar bear mascot, and for an outrageous price I got my picture taken with him. I found that picture recently and I am embarrassed anyone had to be seen with me like that.

Years later, you went to California for a year to learn Russian and take some other college classes. You spoke to me a few times while you were there (about writing this book I believe). I regret not going when you invited me. I wish I would have taken advantage of traveling more when I had the chance.

Playing Crusader with you and Dad was always fun. It got a little redundant after a while so I gave it a break, but I do miss it some days. I'm glad you enjoy the game so much and that I showed it to you and Dad. Unfortunately you're both better than me now. I never stand a chance when I play against you two unless Dad cheats and helps me out, which happens a lot in case you didn't know. Someday I will beat you fair and square.

Up until recently we never talked much. I seem to have this problem with all of my siblings. It's okay though, I understand. Sometimes you just have nothing to say to your 14 year old sister when you're 26. Personality wise I'd say we have the most in common out of the four of us. Same general interests, same facial features (to an extent,) and the same sense of humor. If Dad is in the room everyone always gets a kick out of listening to the three of us laugh in the same deep monotone voice.

To be honest with you, I was upset to learn that you had gotten remarried. I didn't even know you had a divorce. I love your new wife, definitely an upgrade. I'm just hurt that I had to find out about her through Facebook wedding photos. Why didn't you ever tell us?

Even if our relationship is a bit more professional than I would prefer, I'm glad you're actually a part of my life now, instead of a stranger I get to see every Thanksgiving.

-*Meghan*

Dear Little Sis,

We never got to spend the kind of time together like I wanted, yet we know each other very well. I remember playing with you when you were still a toddler and the times when Dad made me entertain you before you grew older, before I left, before we all left. I was a fair-sky visitor back then, to all that would have me, and I have continued that mantra all these years, forever coming, always going. Time has never been on my side in this regard, which I shall address later. I do obtain within my dark soul another memory of you, one of guilt. I met you and your mother at the Bronx Zoo and we went around visiting the animals. That is, of course, what people do at the zoo, right? My memories are all trashed. I only know what people tell me. I was probably hung over or high, probably smelled of cheap girls and cigarettes. I likely attempted to hide these things as we snapped that picture together but my terrible nature came out in that wretched smile upon my face just the same. I was likely a stranger to you in those days, and, as I look at the photo, I was a stranger even to myself.

Your world and my world were very different growing up. You must have been so lonely and I do not envy you in the least. I'll take the loud, messy, dirty, pretend existence with our other sisters any day over being alone in that place. A small town freshly dried of bicycles and madness. This may all seem a tad bleak, especially if you have some fondness in your own memories of me, that I would have none in mine. I think poorly on my own behavior, not that of others, and certainly not that of yours. You were innocent, and in a way, you still are to me. I wanted to be there for you, I wanted to be there for my own brother as well. I wanted to be that large, unwavering rock that guides the younger siblings and cousins towards the path of righteousness as the future patriarch of our family. Like I said, I am a visitor, nothing more, a welcomed guest on the doorstep that stays only long enough for the wine to keep pouring and the dry jokes to continue, a quiet shrill, a comment on society that goes away after the point has been heard. Do you know how many couches I have slept on? No, of course you wouldn't. I now have two couches of my own and I don't sleep on either, funny how that works.

I wasn't there because I am never here. Time is a basket-case, wrapped in gold linen, tumbled into the ocean from a faraway bridge. I live in the future and I worry myself to death over conniving examples of my own existence. I set my own traps, thank you very much, and I do so without looking back, a convenient loss of memories, spilled from a bucket down the trail like sweet red berries.

So, if I don't see our past, yet I seem to still hold an unwavering connection to you, what must lie in our future? Well, only what I am planning, whether you are willing or not. Most are not willing, which has given me uneasiness with regards to people in general. This feeling of loss and betrayal continues to be justified. People disappoint, but I will not, I refuse. Not too long after our meeting at the Bronx Zoo, I began finishing things, addicted to their completion. I even finished forging this gun which conveniently makes these holes in my feet, see? I pride myself in now having the ability to finish what I start, what I say I am going to do. I simply would like to have the honor of teaching you this simple rule. Be a finisher, carry out the deed, no matter how ugly the final product may seem.

You used to make art, why no art now? Or, do you still and am I simply careless? Did the video games and TV eat your brain? They did mine a little. I still have a chunk I am trying to get back but they are so hungry. I want to write with you, carry you onto my black horse as it rides this pipe dream of the true artist's wish: To Be Free. I could see us travel together, see the sights as it were, conquer people with our amazing talents of manipulation. We could use our hungry genetic code to divide and conquer, steal hearts away and make poison. We could be a dynamic duo, but we'll have to start on the page, convince those beggars to listen to our endearing cackle which we two share.

I wish I could live here, amongst the melodrama and the expert of time. I am aloof, standing before you in a haze of forgetfulness, plunged away into some distant sunrise. This, of course, is self-inflicted optimism. I need a partner-in-crime, a confidant for all of these evil deeds I am scheming. You appear to be the best candidate.

-Marc

Self,

You never were a doer. You have always been lazy, a waste of potential. To be fair, you were raised that way. That good enough was all you had to strive for. Why work harder? You didn't need to cook or clean. You had better things to do, like get to the next level on World of Warcraft or see how many hours you could sleep in a row.

You were the baby so you were treated like one. Your siblings before you had to clean every day, they had to pick up after themselves without question or face consequence. But not you, no, make a mess and leave it there. Someone else will pick it up. Eat all the food and drink all the soda, haha! Who cares if you get fat and weigh 200 pounds when you're 15? You are the queen and you can do whatever you want (as long as it's in the house or yard.)

You wasted so many years with your old friend Sadness. The hours poured into somber thought and self-loathing. So many nights spent looking for company to muffle the static of gut wrenching agony.

You are boiling with potential. The years of coddling have poisoned your mind and spirit. You can be free, drink the antidote, suffer from the withdrawal of caffeine and laziness, and reap the reward.

This journey will be complex and unyielding at best. You are already so far behind. You will never be able to make up for the time you've lost, do not look back. You are not that person anymore. Those days are gone, nothing more than a husk, a shell of your former self. There will be times when you will want to give up. There will be challenges that seem to only trek uphill. Well guess what? You wanted a nice ass anyway. Put on your hiking boots, tall socks, and start hiking.

Set your goals and meet them with an incurable yearning for more, even if it's just one more step. Do it, and then do it again. You can surpass every assumption ever made, break every standard set, and lift yourself above every bar that has been set for you. Do everything you've ever dreamt of. Paint, sing, write, and grow. Go back to school. Do the work and do it right. Make your future and your happiness your number one priority. Be strong, speak your mind. Lead and be an inspiration. Be a storm with unmet resilience. You can do and be all these things and so much more. You will not regret it.

Hard work is not in your blood. "You come from a long line of quitters." Maybe this is true. Even if it is, you can create the ethics you long for. Birth them from the ashes of your deceased self, nurture them, and raise them to believe that "good enough" isn't good at all.

-Meghan

Marc,

*L*et us begin.

Is it possible that you will look back in twenty, even thirty years and feel great pride in your undeniable accomplishments? You've got some nerve to imagine that you have established a real thread on your life. For decades you continue to leave a little in the reserve tank, just like that old Harley you used to own that only ran a little. Even while doing pushups for the drill sergeants, even while working on a case, even while being in love. You leave some on the table, just in case. Nestled in your back pocket is your precious, comfortable reserve.

You have yet to give it your all, *just getting by* is your famous motto. And sure, great things have come of this meager effort. In reality, where true great men live only for one moment of their lives, your deeds have only been *good.* You are always doing *good,* you live in the *good.* You peer at easy eyes in the mirror as some kind of leader of the losers, a natural king underdog and you smile. That crown is set well upon your head and has been for years. Not a crown of thorns, not a crown of jewels, but a crown of paper and rare ink. It is easier down there, with them, isn't it? Is it not warmer and kinder to be the leader of the parade of the second class? You love them, and they in turn look up to you. You are a pancreas. You conduct a small function that helps everyone out for the common good but you can be replaced, there isn't a long waiting list.

Being a B+ type of guy that I know you are, I find your lack of motivation to take this life to the next level draining. You settle, are a settler. Why? It's easy in the depths. There is no rat race to be seen. Go ahead, make up for your lack of effort, you do it all the time. There are two methods which we have observed: A whirlwind of sudden brilliance from a high perch that you laze upon. See what I can do? In all second situations, you overcome your laziness with your intellect and confidence man style approach to interpersonal relationships. You can fool all of them out there that think you are just great, think you are working so hard, have achieved so much. You are not fooling us.

Do you honestly believe the great men of the past wasted this much time on leisure? Watching shows at will and playing computer games as some great Japanese warlord until two in the morning has become your alibi. You work all day and this is your savory routine, your reward for being such a *good boy*. You are a consumer of dust. You might as well suck on that cold barrel now and save the electricity or you will end up the same as everyone you know. How common can you be? How much can you blend into the background?

Sure, you can turn on the tap at any time and bleed out the poison that the crowd all loves to hear. Spinning yarn has never been a problem, only the frequency of the wheel. You think to us inside your head that this content just seeps out of your pours, so why sweat so much? Why work out if you already pour gold? Have you ever thought of where your talent comes from? It is us, you fool, all of us together in this poor, dying pouch. You are both naïve and undeserving of what little talent you have. Such a big head, you can do this any time, *so why now? Why sweat it? Why work?* That is because, Dear Friend, you are afraid.

Cowards accept what is given to them and fail to ask questions. They lie in the dark and pity themselves to sleep. Is that you? Could that be us? What a little lizard you are, creeping about, clinging to stalks and branches, how cool you must feel. You cower behind your shield of mediocrity with the ready excuse for failure, "well…I didn't even try and look how far I got."

Actually, we may have you all wrong. Wait, no… could it be? The consensus is in from the parlor crowd, yes, you are afraid of success. All this time, you pull back the last punch because you are afraid the blow might actually land. Success is your secret little vice that you dabble with, your never public after party fix. Yes, always a private drug to do behind closed doors. No real ties, nothing to connect, just a secret relationship that you hope to keep but never make substantiated. Is that why we have so many holes in our feet? Is that why we have gunpowder on our hands? Yes, you are afraid of this subtle mistress, but I tell you that *We are Not.*

From this moment on you have a choice. You can continue down this path of mediocrity, just as you have tended that simple flame of the past. Or, you could achieve true greatness by your own measure. Grasp that comfortable solitude of knowing that you got yours in this life without our outright help. Decide soon, Dear Friend, because there is brewing a revolt in these dark corridors. Soon we will take control and oh how everything will change.

–Marc

About the
Letter Writers

*M*arc **D. Crepeaux** is a curator, editor and writer for *Letters Never Meant to be Read*. Marc has also authored the gritty, Southern crime novel *Modern Waste* and the poetry collection *Worked Stiff: Poetry and Prose for the Common*. He is from Killawog, NY and spent much of his late-teens and early twenties in NYC where he acted like a maniac. He now works as an English teacher and a Captain in the Army Reserves, among other entrepreneurial endeavors, and holds an MFA in Creative Writing. Marc lives in a more calming environment with his wife, two daughters, two dogs, and two fish in Rome, GA. He can be found in excess on marcdcrepeaux.com

*J*oel **Dockery** was born a Yankee in Oregon but has since become a naturalized citizen of the Deep South, though not yet acclimated to the long stretches without rain and the sometime utter lack of snow. He joined the Marines when he was 17 to see the world or, more accurately, to get away. Since then he's tried many adventurous things, including marriage, which provided him with the greatest challenge he'd ever faced-raising children.

For a living Mr. Dockery hikes, hunts, fishes, bikes, makes things, fixes things and constantly searches for further understanding. He does these deeds with his children at times so that they understand that not all enjoyable things are expensive and created by corporations.

*B*randon Lawrence is a musician, songwriter, nerd, lover of all things nerd, and a hobbyist. He loves to delve into new interests as any curious human being. Brandon lives in the deep dark of Pennsylvania where he tends to his goal in life to go above and beyond in an attempt to relate and be relatable. We all need someone, or at the very least, something of someone to relate to. Brandon takes that approach to heart and hopes to achieve that goal with you through his letters.

*M*eghan C. Rynn was born and raised in Central NY and lived through the great flood of 2006. She then traveled north to the frozen tundra and fought in the great battle against the undead. She braved the 10,000 steps only to take an arrow to the knee. Meghan started writing as a child. She drew comics, wrote short stories, and even wrote a movie script later used for a college project. She is the mayor of a small town called Mari-si, and is the Bug-off champion two years running. Meghan works full time as a personal care aid in Central New York where she cares for people with traumatic brain injuries. She is attending college to become a veterinarian by 2024 with hopes of being out of debt before she dies.

66068796R00089

Made in the USA
Charleston, SC
11 January 2017